# CLASSIC ARTS & CRAFTS FURNITURE

## 14 Timeless Designs

by Robert W. Lang

**POPULAR WOODWORKING BOOKS**
CINCINNATI, OHIO
www.popularwoodworking.com

# Table of Contents

*Introduction*      4

## CASEWORK

**Project One**
*Arts & Crafts Buffet*      6

**Project Two**
*Stickley Music Cabinet*      18

*Further: Jig for Through Moritse*      28

*Further: Reinforcing the Indestructible*      30

*Further: When A&C Joinery Becomes Decoration*      32

**Project Three**
*Arts & Crafts Bridal Chest*      34

**Project Four**
*Byrdcliffe Linen Press*      40

**Project Five**
*Greene & Greene Medicine Cabinet*      52

## BOOK STORAGE

**Project Six**
*Craftsman Bookcase*      60

**Project Seven**
*Stickley Book Rack*      70

*Further: Authentic Stickley Finish*      78

**Project Eight**
*Harvey Ellis Bookcase*      80

**Project Nine**
*Tusk Tenon Bookrack*      90

# TABLES & CHAIRS

**Project Ten**
*Greene & Greene Sideboard*      98

**Project Eleven**
*Lost Stickley Side Table*      110

*Further: Slanted View of Moritses*      118

**Project Twelve**
*Stickley Poppy Table*      120

*Further: Living on the Edge*      128

*Further: Hand Tools/Power Tools*      130

**Project Thirteen**
*Gustav Stickley Morris Chair*      132

*Further: Matching Mortise Size*      142

# OTHER

**Project Fourteen**
*Greene & Greene Frame*      144

*In the Greene & Greene Style*      148

*Further: Coping With Curves*      154

*Further: 3-Ways to an Arts & Crafts Finish*      156

# ▶ Introduction

Like many an aspiring woodworker, I found myself drawn to the designs of Gustav Stickley and other Arts & Crafts period makers early on. I dropped out of college in the early 1970s with a desire to find a career where there would be some physical evidence of my efforts at the end of the day. I didn't want to sit in an office and I didn't want to wear a tie. My father advised me to learn a trade so I could, as he put it "pay the bills while you figure out what you want to do".

Instead, I decided to become a musician. But that rebellious decision did lead me to the cabinetmaker's trade. A band mate and I went into business making speaker cabinets for PA systems and I enjoyed the process of making things from wood more than I expected. A few years later, after a stint repairing wooden boats, leading the scenery shop for an aquatic theme park and work in a commercial cabinet shop, I took the plunge and began building furniture as an independent craftsman.

At that time, the resources we enjoy today were few and far between. One of the ways I learned about making furniture was the study of earlier work, and I particularly enjoyed books of measured drawings. As I worked my way through books of Shaker, Chinese and Early American furniture I noticed a lack of resources for what was becoming my favorite style, the American Arts & Crafts period of the early 20th century. I fully expected that someone would someday come along with a book of measured drawings for this style.

Instead, I found a steady stream of magazine articles and books that promised authenticity but delivered "Arts & Crafts Made Easy" or "Almost a Reproduction of One of Those Stickley Guys".

I began digging into the period myself because I felt that this style was important. It was a reaction to the mass-produced junk of the "Golden Oak" period. Gustav Stickley went back to the basics and made chairs, tables and case pieces that served their functions, were beautifully proportioned and were too well made to wear out – a unique style that hadn't been seen before.

This stuff is a wonderful example of the way furniture should be made. As a builder the challenge is to perform the basic tasks of joinery and wood selection well enough that they are worthy of being the focus, not hidden under piles of fancy molding or showy brass. As a designer, the lessons are those of proportion and subtle details. My dissatisfaction with what was being published eventually pushed me into writing the book I would have liked to own when I was started out. My first book "Shop Drawings for Craftsman Furniture" was successful enough that it led to others, and that eventually brought me into my current job on the Popular Woodworking Magazine staff.

In my work at the magazine, I tried to explore the projects that had been overlooked and present methods of building that make exposed joinery approachable and possible. The projects in this book were chosen selfishly; they are pieces I wanted to make for myself, challenges I wanted to take on, and side trips to the less-travelled areas of the Arts & Crafts period. The issues and needs that original pieces of Craftsman furniture addressed are still with us, and making this furniture is an excellent way to both fill your home and let your family and guests know that quality material, sound design and good craftsmanship are still worthy values.

Robert W. Lang, March 2013

# Arts & Crafts Buffet

## Recipe for successful design:
## Steal your ideas from the best.

I designed this buffet cabinet a couple years ago for a weekend seminar on Arts & Crafts joinery. After the class I added a 3-D model to the *Popular Woodworking Magazine* online SketchUp collection. It was an easy way to provide detailed plans for those in attendance. As time passed, the model rose to the top of the collection, based on popularity.

My goal in designing it was to combine several classic elements from the early 20th century, without building a reproduction of any one piece in particular. I was looking to design a piece with a contemporary feel, but was also grounded in traditional Arts & Crafts period elements. Apparently I swiped the right details from the right sources to make a successful piece.

The wide overhanging top with breadboard ends, the finger-jointed drawer and the sculpted handles were all borrowed from the designs of Charles and Henry Greene. The proportions of the door stiles and rails were lifted right from the Gustav Stickley stylebook, and the double-tapered legs are a Harvey Ellis element turned upside down.

Equally important are the overall proportions and the rounded edges that ease the transitions where there is a change of direction or a change in plane. The light color of the soft maple keeps the cabinet from looking too formal or too masculine. Absent are the elements often seen in new pieces based on old designs. Corbels and spindles were banished to the land of overused and misapplied design features.

Classic combination. This buffet has a contemporary feel, but it is a combination of classic design elements of the American Arts & Crafts period of the early 20th century.

## Skinny Legs & All

The legs are important visually; the upward taper leads the eye to the top, and the wide portion near the bottom makes the base appear substantial. Combined with the wide rails on the bottom of the doors, the case sits on a firm visual foundation, and it looks larger and heavier than it really is.

The legs are also key elements in the structure. Each leg is a corner for two different frames. There is a lot of joinery in each, and to help keep track of the leg locations, I laid out the tapers after resawing the legs from 8/4 stock. My local supplier didn't have material available to simply mill the legs to the 1¼" finished dimension, so I bought thicker than I needed, resawed the boards to 1⅜" and saved the thin offcuts for the bottom of the drawer.

My method is to work out all the joinery first, then cut pieces to shape and round the edges just before final assembly. I cut the ⅜"-wide stopped grooves for the side and back panels first, using a plunge router. I then lowered the depth setting and cut the mortises in the wide faces of the legs with the same router.

There isn't enough of a flat area on the narrow sides of the legs to support the router, so I moved to the hollow-chisel mortiser to add the mortises for the front and back rails. Then I cut the tenons on the ends of the top and bottom side rails. I used a backsaw for the shoulder cuts, then cut the cheeks on the band saw.

I dry-fit the side rails to the legs, forming side sub-assemblies without panels. Then I made the joints for the front and back rails. In the back, the mortises fall within the grooves for the back panel. In the front of the case, the mortises are the only joinery.

To keep the backs of the front and back rails flush with the back of the legs, I set my marking gauge directly to the edge of a mortise. Then I used that setting to mark out the tenons. I cut the tenon shoulders with my backsaw and the cheeks on the band saw. After fitting these joints, I did another dry run, connecting the two side assemblies with the front and back rails.

## Come Together

With a complex piece such as this, the best way to ensure that everything fits together is to make careful dry runs, then pull the actual dimensions for the next piece to be fabricated from the subassembly. With the legs connected side to side and front to back, I made sure the carcase was square before making the bottom.

The bottom fits between the front and back rails, and at the ends there is a pair of through-tenons. The critical distance is from shoulder to shoulder on these tenons. After ripping the

*Better than numbers. Setting the marking gauge directly to the edge of the mortise ensures exact alignment of the rail and leg.*

*When to stop. When a corner can be forced into the mortise, the thickness is close. Then it's time to cut the edges of the tenons.*

bottom to width, I held the bottom in place below the rails on the carcase and marked the shoulder locations directly.

Then it all came back apart to cut the through-mortises in the bottom side rails. These pieces are too short to clamp to the bench and have room for the plunge router, and too wide to fit easily in the mortiser. I drilled out the bulk of the waste with a Forstner bit at the drill press, then cleaned up the mortises with chisels and a float.

The first step in making the tenons was to cut a wide rabbet on both the top and bottom of the shelf. I clamped a straight-edge on the shoulder line and used a router with a straight bit and a top-mounted flush guide bearing.

I made a cut on both ends on the top side, then I clamped the straightedge on the bottom. I carefully made a cut, then

*Knowledge is power. Measuring with calipers reveals the exact thickness of the tenon and how far to set the depth of the router bit.*

*Where it belongs. Marking the tenons directly from the mortises is faster and far more accurate than measuring.*

*Easier by hand. These cuts could be made at the table saw, but that would be an awkward operation. Cutting the tenons by hand allows me to see what is going on.*

measured the thickness of the tenon, comparing it to the height of the mortise. When I could force a corner of the bottom into the mortise, I knew I was as close as I wanted to come with the router.

I held the backside of the rail against the end of the cabinet bottom and marked the ends of the tenons from the mortises. I cut the ends of the tenons with my backsaw, then turned the bottom 90° and used the same tool to make the two end cuts. I used a jigsaw to remove the material between the tenons and stayed about ⅛" away from the shoulder's edge.

There is just enough material from the first router cut that defines the shoulder to guide the bearing of a flush-trim router bit. That took care of making a straight edge between the tenons, except for a small quarter circle in the corners. A little chisel work removed that extra material, and I was ready to test the fit.

With a chisel, I cut a small chamfer around the back edges of the mortises, and I used my block plane to chamfer the ends of the tenons. A few taps with a mallet revealed the tight spots on the tenons. Some work with a shoulder plane and float brought the tenons down to size, and after achieving a good fit with both rails on the ends of the bottom, I was ready to dry-fit the rest of the case.

## Shapes of Things

After another test-fit and a bit of tweaking, I was ready for a break from joinery, so I cut the tapers on the legs at the band saw. I cleaned up the saw marks with a light pass across the jointer, then began smoothing surfaces and rounding edges. I began smoothing all the flat surfaces with a plane to remove mill marks and evidence of beatings from my test assemblies.

I took my cue for the edge treatment from Greene & Greene. Instead of running a roundover bit in a router around the edges, I used my block plane to hand-form a radius on all the exposed edges. This doesn't take as long as you might think, and this method allows for variation of the edge radius.

The radius on the legs is larger at the bottom than at the top. This follows the taper of the legs and adds a subtlety to

*Why this slides. Opening the mouth of the block plane provides room to skew the iron.*

*Big mouth, quick work. This side of the plane will take a coarse cut, removing a lot of material in a hurry.*

*Fine on this side. The other side of the plane takes a small finishing cut. The amount of material removed and the quality of cut is controlled by moving the plane laterally.*

*Dry-fit now, panels later. The only way to know if things will really fit is to put the carcase together. The panels will be added the next time around.*

the edges that a router couldn't provide. My method for doing this efficiently is to open wide the mouth of my block plane and skew the blade as far as I can.

With the blade cocked, the plane takes a big bite on one side and a fine cut on the other. By shifting the position of the plane as I tilt it on the edge of the board, I can remove a large chamfered edge to begin the cut, then make fine finishing cuts to remove the arrises and form a nice curve. Shifting the position of the plane laterally allows it to do coarse, medium and fine work without fiddling with the tool.

I also cut the arches at the bottom edge of the front and side rails at the band saw, and used a series of rasps to refine the curves and round the edges. I made ⅝"-thick panels for the sides, making a rabbet around the perimeter to form a tongue on the panel that fits in the grooves of the legs.

Then I made ⅜"-thick shiplapped panels for the back before turning to the last bit of joinery for the case. A simple web frame supports the drawer, and two rails (one at the front and one at the back behind the visible rails) support the top.

The web frame is mortise-and-tenon construction; I assembled and fit this frame with the cabinet dry-assembled. I put the cabinet together and took it apart several times to fit parts as the joinery progressed to ensure that the complex assembly

would all fit together. And it served as good practice for the final glue-up.

I cut the two top rails to the outside width of the case and marked the inside edges to the top side rails. I made a ¼"-wide rabbet on the bottom of the ends, then cut a dovetail on both ends of each rail. With the rails in position, I marked the top side rails to cut the sockets.

I used a wheel marking gauge to mark the bottom of the dovetail sockets in the rails and a knife to mark the vertical

# Arts & Crafts Buffet

| NO. | ITEM | DIMENSIONS (INCHES) | | | MATERIAL | COMMENTS |
|---|---|---|---|---|---|---|
| | | T | W | L | | |
| ☐ 4 | Legs | $1\frac{1}{4}$ | $3\frac{3}{4}$ | $30\frac{3}{4}$ | Maple | |
| ☐ 2 | Upper side rails | $\frac{7}{8}$ | 3 | $13\frac{3}{8}$ | Maple | $\frac{3}{4}$" TBE* |
| ☐ 2 | Lower side rails | $\frac{7}{8}$ | $4\frac{1}{4}$ | $13\frac{3}{8}$ | Maple | $\frac{3}{4}$" TBE |
| ☐ 2 | Side panels | $\frac{5}{8}$ | $12\frac{5}{8}$ | $23\frac{1}{2}$ | Maple | |
| ☐ 1 | Cabinet bottom | $\frac{7}{8}$ | $11\frac{7}{8}$ | $30\frac{1}{4}$ | Maple | $1\frac{1}{4}$" TBE |
| ☐ 6 | Back panels | $\frac{3}{8}$ | $4\frac{7}{8}$ | $23\frac{1}{2}$ | Maple | Shiplap edges |
| ☐ 1 | Upper back rail | $\frac{7}{8}$ | 3 | 27 | Maple | $1\frac{1}{4}$" TBE |
| ☐ 2 | Lower front/back rails | $\frac{7}{8}$ | $4\frac{1}{4}$ | 27 | Maple | $1\frac{1}{4}$" TBE |
| ☐ 1 | Top front rail | $\frac{7}{8}$ | $\frac{7}{8}$ | 27 | Maple | $1\frac{1}{4}$" TBE |
| ☐ 1 | Front drawer rail | $\frac{7}{8}$ | $1\frac{1}{4}$ | 27 | Maple | $1\frac{1}{4}$" TBE |
| ☐ 2 | Inner top rails | $\frac{3}{4}$ | 3 | $29\frac{1}{2}$ | Maple | DTBE** |
| ☐ 2 | Web frame rails | $\frac{3}{4}$ | $2\frac{1}{4}$ | $23\frac{3}{4}$ | Poplar | $1\frac{1}{4}$" TBE |
| ☐ 2 | Web frame stiles | $\frac{3}{4}$ | $3\frac{1}{4}$ | $11\frac{7}{8}$ | Poplar | |
| ☐ 2 | Hinge strips | $\frac{1}{2}$ | 1 | $18\frac{7}{8}$ | Maple | |
| ☐ 2 | Door hinge stiles | $\frac{7}{8}$ | $3\frac{5}{8}$ | $18\frac{7}{8}$ | Maple | |
| ☐ 2 | Door lock stiles | $\frac{7}{8}$ | $2\frac{7}{8}$ | $18\frac{7}{8}$ | Maple | |
| ☐ 2 | Door top rails | $\frac{7}{8}$ | $3\frac{3}{8}$ | $7\frac{3}{4}$ | Maple | $1\frac{1}{4}$" TBE |
| ☐ 2 | Door bottom rails | $\frac{7}{8}$ | $4\frac{5}{8}$ | $7\frac{3}{4}$ | Maple | $1\frac{1}{4}$" TBE |
| ☐ 2 | Door panels | $\frac{5}{8}$ | 6 | $11\frac{5}{8}$ | Maple | |
| ☐ 1 | Top | $\frac{3}{4}$ | $15\frac{7}{8}$ | $46\frac{1}{2}$ | Maple | $1\frac{1}{4}$" TBE |
| ☐ 2 | Breadboard ends | $\frac{7}{8}$ | $2\frac{1}{4}$ | $16\frac{1}{8}$ | Maple | |
| ☐ 2 | Drawer sides | $\frac{3}{4}$ | $4\frac{3}{4}$ | 13 | Maple | |
| ☐ 1 | Drawer front | $\frac{3}{4}$ | $4\frac{3}{4}$ | $24\frac{1}{2}$ | Maple | |
| ☐ 1 | Drawer back | $\frac{3}{4}$ | $4\frac{1}{4}$ | $24\frac{1}{2}$ | Maple | |
| ☐ 1 | Drawer bottom | $\frac{1}{4}$ | 12 | $23\frac{1}{2}$ | Maple | |
| ☐ 1 | Drawer handle | $1\frac{1}{4}$ | $1\frac{1}{2}$ | 16 | Maple | |
| ☐ 2 | Door handles | $1\frac{1}{4}$ | $1\frac{3}{4}$ | 5 | Maple | |

*TBE = Tenon both ends; **DTBE = Dovetail both ends*

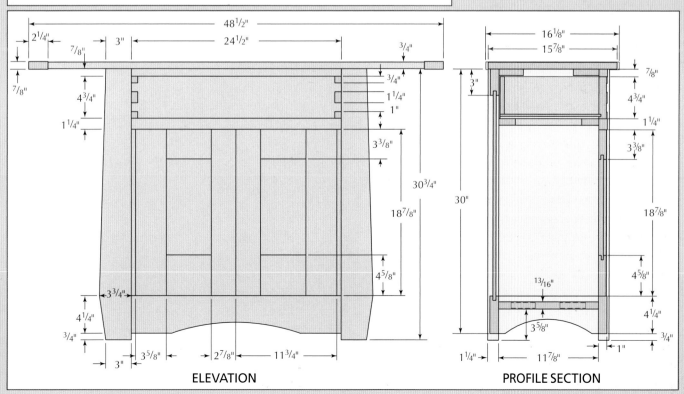

ELEVATION          PROFILE SECTION

*Sliding home. Start all the mortises and get the parts close with a rubber mallet. A few clamps close the joints side to side.*

No-spread zone. A single through-dovetail on each of the top rails locks the sides of the case together and adds an attractive detail.

cuts. After sawing the outside edges with my dovetail saw, I used a chisel to remove the waste (vertical saw cuts into the waste may make waste removal easier). On a small joint such as this, the marking gauge can be used as a small router, providing a flat bottom for the socket.

## Tighten Up

Fighting off the urge to glue the entire box together, I went over all the parts with a card scraper then fine sandpaper. Then I put the side panels in place and glued the rails between the legs, then let these subassemblies dry overnight. This simplified the final assembly by reducing the number of parts. The obvious tricky part of putting things together for real is down low. The through-tenons for the cabinet bottoms need to slide through the mortises in the rail at the same time the tenons in the front and back rails go into the legs. I put the entire cabinet together without any glue to practice my technique and to avoid any trauma during the real thing.

The other tricky part is that, with the legs tapered, there isn't a good surface to place any clamps. Fortunately one of my bad habits was ready to provide a solution. I rarely throw anything away, so I found the tapered offcuts from the legs over by the band saw. Good old blue painter's tape held these to the legs, providing a flat place to put the clamps.

I put one of the side assemblies on my bench with the inside of the case facing up, applied glue to the mortises and put the

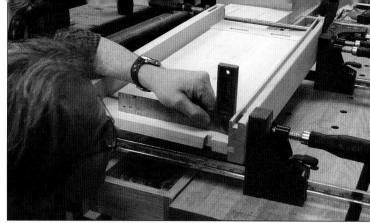

E pluribus unum. Subassemblies minimize the number of pieces to contend with during the final assembly. After clamping, check to see that they are square.

Where bottom and side collide. This isn't as hard as it looks; the side will be one piece, and trial runs ensure that everything fits.

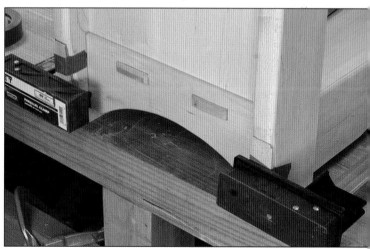

Tape for the tapers. Offcuts from tapering the legs are taped in place to provide a flat surface for the clamps.

rails in place. I started the tenons on the end of the bottom into the side rail mortises, then brushed glue on the inner portion of the tenons. This kept the glue off the exposed ends of the tenons. That was the easy end.

I slid the shiplapped back panels into position, then brushed glue on the tenons in the rails before I started the through-

Simple fix. A pocket screw at each end attaches the drawer frame to the inside of the back legs.

L of a solution. A simple jig attached to the table saw's miter gauge supports the work and indicates the exact line of the cut.

Balancing act. After cutting the first set of fingers, place the end of a side on the drawer front to mark the matching parts of the joint.

tenons into the mortises in the lower side rail. At the same time, I lined up the other tenons with their matching mortises. I tapped down on the rail until all but about ½" of the through-tenon was visible between the tenon shoulder and the rail.

I reached in to brush more glue on the tenons, then tapped on the outside of the side subassembly to close the joints. I tried to tap directly over each tenon on the legs as the second side of the cabinet moved into place. When the side was about ⅛" away from closing, I put down the mallet and picked up my cabinet clamps.

I tightened the clamps and went on a hunt for glue squeeze-out near the joints. I try to control squeeze-out by applying just enough glue to the joint. The goal is to apply the glue so that it almost squeezes out. The last step in the carcase assembly was to jockey the web frame into position and glue the long edge to the rail below the drawer opening. At the back, a couple pocket screws from below attach the back of the frame to the back legs.

I had a little glue bead appear here and there, and those were scraped off with the back of a sharp, wide chisel before the glue had time to dry. I keep a wet rag handy to keep the chisel clean and don't wipe the wood unless I have to.

## Feeling Groovy

The doors are standard frame-and-panel construction; ¼"-wide grooves run along the inside edges, and haunched tenons in the rails fit mortises in the stiles. The elements of the doors are all wider than they need to be. This enhances the overall appearance of the doors in the opening; there is a better balance in the middle, and the wide lower rails reinforce the sense of visual weight toward the bottom of the cabinet.

The combined width of the doors is 1" less than the width of the opening; thin strips are glued inside the legs to carry the hinges. This detail allows the doors to be set back from the front edges of the rails while still able to swing freely past the inside edges of the legs. These features are common in Gustav Stickley designs. The variation of planes adds visual interest to the unadorned surfaces.

The drawer is joined at the front with Greene & Greene-style finger joints. The fingers are graduated in width, and they extend about ⅛" past the drawer front. I made a simple L-shaped fixture and attached it to the table saw's miter gauge to assist in cutting the joints. After attaching the fixture, I ran it through the saw blade to cut a slot in the lower portion.

I laid out the fingers on one of the drawer sides, making sure to clearly mark the waste area. Then I adjusted the height

*Cutting corners. Mark where the end of the drawer side intersects the fingers on the drawer front. Round over the edges to the pencil line.*

*Room to move. Elongate the sides of the holes that pass through the tenons. This will allow the top to expand and contract against the breadboard ends.*

*Adjustable guide. The drawer guides are glued to the web frame. The short length and rabbeted bottom edge provide room to adjust the width with a block plane.*

of the blade to match the marked depth of the cut between the fingers. I placed the two drawer sides together and aligned the pencil marks on the wood with the saw cut in the fixture.

When the sides were in position, I clamped the stacked sides to the back of the fixture. I cut the ends of each finger before removing the waste material in between. When the sides were finished, I placed them on each end of the drawer front to transfer the cutlines.

After marking the waste area in the drawer front joints, I lowered the height of the saw blade to leave the ends of the drawer front barely proud of the drawer sides. I then cut the fingers in the drawer front in the same way that I cut the mating ends of the drawer sides.

When I was happy with the joints at the front of the drawer, I cut grooves with a small plunge router in the sides and front for the drawer bottom. The grooves in the sides stop at the front to match the depth of the groove in the drawer front. The groove falls within the first finger, so it can run from end to end through the drawer front.

The back of the drawer is narrower than the sides. It comes down from the top of the drawer and ends at the top of the groove, allowing the drawer bottom to be slid into place after the drawer is assembled. The drawer bottom is one solid panel, glued up from the leg leftovers and planed to 1/4" thickness. The back and sides of the drawer are joined with through-dovetails.

## Roundabout

Like the cabinet it lives in, the drawer was put together and taken back apart several times. With the sides in place, I marked the front edge of the drawer front on the fingers of the drawer sides. This provided a target for rounding the edges of the fingers. I clamped the sides in my vise and went to work with a small rasp.

As with the other radiused edges, I began by cutting a 45°

*One-two punch. Locate the punch and smack it a couple times with a hammer. This cuts sharp corners and straight sides for the plug hole.*

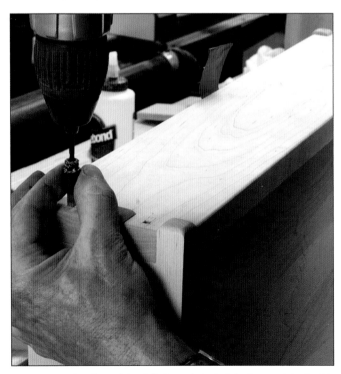

*Waste removal: Follow with a drill through the hole in the punch body. This removes the waste within the square recess.*

chamfer, working in the direction of the grain. When the edge of the chamfer reached about two-thirds of the distance from the end to the pencil line, I removed the sharp edges and began to transform the faceted edges to a gentle curve. When I got close to the lines, I switched to a piece of #180-grit Abranet to remove the rasp marks.

I didn't want any glue to squeeze out when I assembled the drawer, so I carefully applied glue to the recesses between the fingers with an acid brush. I began with the end-grain surfaces, let the glue soak in for a few minutes, then applied glue to all the mating surfaces. I clamped the drawer box together at the front, placing small blocks of scrap between the fingers to provide a bearing surface for the clamps.

I planed the bottom edge of the drawer front before assembly to keep the edge of the front 1/16" above the bottom edge of the sides. When I fit the drawer in the opening, I was able to plane the sides to get a good fit and keep a slight gap between the drawer front and the case rails. Drawer guides are glued on to the web frame to keep the drawer sliding straight. A rabbet on the bottom edge of the guide allowed me to reach in with a block plane to tweak the fit.

## Speaking in Tongues

The breadboard ends have a ¼"-wide, ½"-deep groove along each inside edge. I made each groove with a straight bit in a small plunge router, stopping the groove about 1" in from the ends. I located the matching tongue on the top by clamping a plywood straightedge to the line, and made the cut with a flush-trim bit in the router.

The tongue is 1¼" long; the extra ¾" was used to make three tenons to hold the breadboard in place. The tenons are about 2" wide; the outer tenons end about ⅛" in from the end of the groove. After cutting the tenons, I marked their locations on the breadboard and cut the mortises with the hollow chisel mortiser.

The middle mortise fits the tenon tightly in width, but the end two were cut wider to give the top some room to move. These joints are pinned with square walnut plugs that go completely through the breadboard and the tenons. The square holes for the ¼" and 5⁄16" plugs we made with punches developed by Darrell Peart. These punches work in conjunction with a drill bit, so it was simple to start from the show side, punch the square and drill the holes through the assembled joint.

After drilling, I took the joint apart and placed the drill bit in each hole, then used the punch to square the sides. I elongated the holes in the two outer tenons so they could move in the mortises as the seasons change. On final assembly of the top, I applied glue to the center tenon only. The outer joints are held in place with pegs.

## Maxwell's Silver Hammer

I also added decorative pegs (3⁄16", ¼" and 5⁄16") to the joint locations on the front legs, the door stiles and the drawer front. Recesses of about ¼" deep for the plugs were made with the square punches. The plugs were ripped from some quartersawn walnut. I cut square strips on the table saw, about 1⁄32" larger than the recesses.

I smoothed the long edges of these strips with my block plane, and I measured the width and thickness with calipers until they were close in size, but still a bit larger than the holes. I dropped the end extension of the calipers into the holes to find the correct length for the pegs, then used the jaws of the calipers to transfer this measurement to the strips.

I rounded one end of each strip with a coarse file, followed by sandpaper, before cutting the pegs to length. After cutting, I used a chisel to chamfer the back edges of the pegs to make it easier to start them in the holes. After the pegs were sanded, I treated them with a solution of vinegar in which I'd soaked iron, then cut them to length. This solution reacts with the tannic acid in the walnut and turns the wood black. (Brian Boggs explains an alternative ebonizing process in the June 2009 issue of Popular Woodworking (#176).)

I used an artist's brush to coat the inside of each hole with glue, inserted a peg and tapped it in place with a brass hammer. The smooth hard surface of the hammer burnished the faces of the pegs.

Because the doors hang on strips glued to the inside of the door opening, mortising the hinges was simple. I trimmed the doors to 3⁄32" less than the height of the opening and cut the strips to an exact fit. I put a door (hinge stile up) in my vise and placed a strip along the edge, using a dime to space the top of the strip with the top of the door.

Then I marked the locations of the hinges. I cut the hinge mortises in the doors with a small plunge router equipped with a fence. I put a block of wood behind the door and adjusted the position of the door in the vise so that the edge of the door was flush with the top of the block. This kept the base of the router flat on the thin edge without any danger of tipping.

The mortises in the hinge strips were cut with the strips clamped flat to the benchtop. After routing, I squared the corners of the mortises then screwed the hinges in position on the doors and on the strips. Then I removed the hinges, and glued the strips to the inside of the legs, with the back of the strips flush with the back of the legs.

I glued a small block of wood behind the rail of the face frame above the doors to provide a place to mount brass ball catches to keep the doors shut. The handles were shaped at the band saw, then the edges were rounded with a block plane and rasps. I made relief cuts on the back of the handles with a carving gouge to provide a finger grip. Those cuts were refined with a gooseneck scraper.

The first coat of finish is clear shellac. I used the canned stuff from the hardware store and thinned it about 30 percent. This left the color a bit cold to my eye, so I added about 25 percent amber shellac to the mix for the second, third and fourth coats. After letting the shellac dry, I buffed the surface with a nylon abrasive pad, then applied a coat of paste wax.

## Supplies

**Lee Valley**
leevalley.com | 800-871-8158

1 set ▶ square hole punches
#50K59.20, $26.50-$28.50 each,
$139 for set of six

2 ▶ ball catches
#00W12.00, $1.80 each

*Prices correct at time of publication.*

# Stickley Music Cabinet

## A harmonious combination of details and materials.

One hundred years ago, when people wanted to listen to music at home, they cracked their knuckles and headed for the piano. This small cabinet was originally intended to store sheet music, and although times have changed, it is a nice, small-scale piece of furniture.

The overall form is appealing, and much of the charm is in the details. The exposed through-tenons in the cabinet often are seen in Gustav Stickley furniture, but the joinery in the door is unusual. The mitered intersections on the door are authentic to early Stickley pieces, but within a few years these joints disappeared from production.

I found three variations of the joinery at the outer stiles: full miters, partial miters and butt joints. I chose partial miters to maximize the holding power of the joints while retaining at least some of the look. I couldn't find an original example of this cabinet with that detail, but I included it in this project because it adds to the charm and presence of this piece. It was also an interesting and challenging exercise in joinery.

## Making a Mitered Mullion Door

The obvious solution, mitering individual pieces, would have little strength and no built-in way to keep the parts aligned. The miters are for show; unseen joints provide strength and alignment. Mortises and tenons are used behind the miters at the intersections at the outer stiles.

In the middle, there isn't enough room in the 1¼"-wide stile to include a practical mortise-and-tenon joint. My solution was a modified lap joint; the miters are cut down to where the rabbet for the glass begins, and the back part of the short pieces simply butt against the center stile.

The matching cutouts in the center stile prevent the ends of the muntins from moving out of place and provide some face-grain-to-face-grain glue surface. It's stronger than you might think. The tricky part is getting the four points of each joint to meet neatly in the middle.

Careful layout is essential, and I began by clamping the three stiles together so I could mark them all at once. I set the vertical distance between the muntins on my combination square, and used the square to step off the spaces. After marking each space, I use a scrap of muntin stock held against the square to mark the width of those parts.

Before working on the miters, I cut a rabbet for the glass, leaving ¼" of material at the face. I used the back of a chisel to clean the corners of the rabbets, then I made ¼"-wide by 1¼"-deep mortises aligned with the rabbet at the muntin location on the outer stiles, and upper and lower rails.

## The Fussy Part

I marked off the miters with my combination square on the vertical mullion, by drawing two pencil lines to form an "X." For the joints to look good, the end of the miters need to meet at a single point. To preserve the points, I used my knife to mark just inside the pencil lines on each side of the mullion.

My first plan was to make a template and form the mitered cutouts with a router. After a couple test joints, I decided that the router alone would be too risky. Quartersawn white oak is tenacious stuff and tends to break off in big chunks when it's routed. In addition, the router would leave a rounded surface at the very point that would need to be chiseled to a sharp point.

I used a fine toothed dovetail saw to establish straight, clean lines at the edges of the joints. I added a couple thicknesses of veneer to the fence of the template to move it out from the cut lines. The router, equipped with a bearing above the ⁹⁄₁₆"-diameter straight cutter, left a flat surface at each joint; a chisel was used to trim back to the finished joint lines made by the saw.

The mating pieces were made by first cutting a square

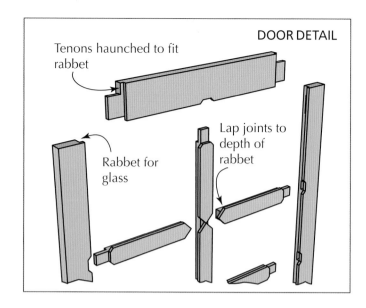

DOOR DETAIL

Tenons haunched to fit rabbet

Rabbet for glass

Lap joints to depth of rabbet

*Better than numbers. A combination square does an excellent job of laying out repeating spaces, in this case the openings in the door.*

*The real thing. A scrap of muntin stock is held against the square to mark the stiles. This speeds the process and ensures accuracy.*

*Run in reverse. The back of a chisel makes a great scraper, just the ticket for cleaning out the corner of rabbets.*

Step back and consider. The router jig is mainly to provide a flat bottom for the lap joint. Set the fence to keep the bit on the waste side of the saw cuts.

Simple setup. Set the fence on the mortiser by lining up the chisel with the back of the rabbet.

shoulder on the back, with a ⅝"-long lap. I marked the miters from the intersection of the shoulder and lap, using my knife and combination square. I sawed outside the lines with a dovetail saw, the used a shooting board with my block plane to fit each joint.

This isn't as tedious as it sounds. It comes down to marking clean lines, cutting as close as possible to them, then testing the fit. Two pieces of wood against each other will tell you where to take another swipe or two on the shooting board. And with the number of joints in this door, there are plenty of opportunities to practice. By the time you get to the last joint, you'll know how to work these joints efficiently.

## The Other End

At the other end of the cross pieces, the mitered corners go back only to the edge of the rabbet, and a tenon is added. After marking the cuts in the stiles with a marking gauge and knife, I put together another simple router jig. I made the jig to fall inside the layout lines, and nibbled away at the thin part of the stile with a flush trim bit.

This jig served double duty. After routing, I reclamped the jig directly on the cut lines and used it to guide my chisel in paring the openings. The other half of the joint was made on

X marks the spot. The joints in the central mullion meet in the exact center. A knife cut along the lines will help to guide the saw.

On the right side. For the points of the miters to meet, the saw cuts must be on opposite sides of the lines on each side of the mullion.

the face of the muntin by first cutting the square shoulder by hand. Then I used the bandsaw to cut the tenon cheeks.

I carefully made a 45° cut in the fence of my bench hook, and used that to guide my saw for the short miter cuts. I left the mortises a bit wide so that I could move the muntins laterally if needed while fitting. After getting the cheeks to fit by filing them with a joinery float, I trimmed the mitered edges with my shoulder plane until they matched the joints in the stiles.

After fitting each joint individually, I made a dry-run assembly of the entire door. There were a couple places that needed tweaking, and I gathered clamps and reviewed my strategy. A lot of joints needed to come together at once, and I didn't want to set myself up to panic in the midst of it.

I gathered my clamps, made some battens to hold the joints flat, then got out an acid brush and a bottle of liquid hide glue. I brushed glue on all of the end-grain surfaces, and allowed the slow-setting glue to wick in. Then I went over the parts again, and brushed glue on the tenons.

I placed one of the outer stiles on its edge, and began placing the tenons of the cross pieces. With the four short muntins in place, I assembled the top and bottom rails to the central mullion, then placed the rail tenons in the mortises of the stile. With the door still on edge, the remaining muntins were placed, followed by the second stile.

I laid the assembly flat on some blocks on the bench and began clamping. The major joints, where the top and bottom rails connect were first. Then I clamped a packing-tape cov-

Cutting corners. The router will leave material in the corner, which can be removed with a chisel. The finished edges of the joint have been established with the knife and saw.

Double duty. This jig guides the bearing on a flush-trim router bit, then is used to guide a chisel to pare into the mitered corners.

ered batten across each of the center miter joints and snugged the clamps. When all the battens were in place, I used bar clamps to bring the ends of the miters together.

I went over the assembly (grateful for the long open time of liquid hide glue) and checked each inside corner for square, and tightened the clamps. I left the door in the clamps overnight, and the following morning, I scraped off the excess glue then leveled the surfaces with my block plane.

## There Is a Cabinet, Too

The cabinet assembly is simple, especially when compared to the door; it's just two sides and an identical top and bottom. After assembly, a backsplash is added behind and above the top, and a narrow toe rail is added below the bottom. The back is a framed panel that fits in a rabbet at the back of the sides. The back panel is flush with the bottom edge of the cabinet bottom, and ends at the midpoint of the top in thickness.

My first step was to cut the rabbets for the back in the sides. This differentiated the inside from the outside and the top from the bottom. The horizontal cabinet components join the sides with a pair of through-tenons at each intersection. I made a template from $1/2$"-thick birch plywood to keep the mortises consistent in size and location.

The template locates the mortises and defines the shape at the top and bottom of the cabinet sides. I chose a piece as wide as the finished sides, and long enough to contain the mortises. To expedite making the template, I ripped some plywood to $1/2$", the width of the finished mortises. I marked the mortise locations on the template blank, then placed double-sided tape over the layout lines.

I stuck down the thin plywood strips at the end of the mortise locations, then placed wider pieces of plywood tight against the long edges. When all these pieces were in place, I tapped them with a mallet to set the adhesive on the tape, then drilled a $7/16$"-diameter hole in each mortise location.

These holes are smaller than the mortise, but larger than the flush-trimming router bit I used to cut out the mortises. After routing all four mortises with a flush-trim bit, I popped off the thin plywood pieces, then cut and shaped the top and bottom edges of the template.

I laid out the mortise locations on the outer faces of the cabinet sides, marking the lines with a knife. The knife lines can't be rubbed off and are more precise and easier to see than pencil lines. More important, these lines are the finished edges of the through-mortises; cutting them first helps to keep the router from tearing out the edge and provides a definite point to work to.

I didn't bother to square the corners of the mortises in the template; the router bit will leave a rounded corner in the cabinet side anyway. I like to drill out as much material as possible before routing, and use the smallest diameter flush-trim bit I can find. Squaring the corners on the real thing looks impossibly difficult, but there are a couple tricks that make it easy.

Use the fence. Saw cuts in the fence of the bench hook guide the saw to make clean and accurate cuts.

Wasting away. The band saw fence is set to leave just a sliver of material as the tenon cheeks are cut.

# Stickley No. 70 Music Cabinet

| | NO. | ITEM | DIMENSIONS (INCHES) | | | MATERIAL | COMMENTS |
|---|---|---|---|---|---|---|---|
| | | | T | W | L | | |
| ❑ | 2 | Case side | $^{13}/_{16}$ | 16 | 46 | QSWO* | |
| ❑ | 2 | Case top & bottom | $^{13}/_{16}$ | 15 | $20^5/_8$ | QSWO | |
| ❑ | 1 | Backsplash | $^7/_8$ | $3^7/_{16}$ | $18^3/_8$ | QSWO | |
| ❑ | 1 | Toe rail | $^{13}/_{16}$ | $1^7/_8$ | $18^1/_4$ | QSWO | |
| ❑ | 2 | Door stiles | $^{13}/_{16}$ | $1^7/_8$ | $37^7/_8$ | QSWO | |
| ❑ | 1 | Door top rail | $^{13}/_{16}$ | $2^1/_2$ | $16^1/_4$ | QSWO | $1^1/_4$" TBE** |
| ❑ | 1 | Door bottom rail | $^{13}/_{16}$ | 3 | $16^1/_4$ | QSWO | $1^1/_4$" TBE |
| ❑ | 1 | Door mullion | $^{13}/_{16}$ | $1^1/_4$ | $34^7/_8$ | QSWO | 1" TBE |
| ❑ | 8 | Door muntins | $^{13}/_{16}$ | $1^1/_4$ | $7^7/_8$ | QSWO | 1" TOE*** |
| ❑ | 2 | Hinge stiles | $^{13}/_{16}$ | $1^5/_8$ | $37^7/_8$ | QSWO | Rabbet long edge |
| ❑ | 40 | Glass stops | $^1/_4$ | $^7/_{16}$ | 7 | QSWO | Cut to fit openings |
| ❑ | 10 | Glass | $^1/_8$ | $5^7/_8$ | $6^5/_8$ | Glass | Cut to fit openings |
| ❑ | 4 | Shelves | $^{13}/_{16}$ | $14^1/_4$ | $18^1/_8$ | QSWO | |
| ❑ | 2 | Back panel stiles | $^3/_4$ | $4^1/_2$ | $39^1/_8$ | QSWO | |
| ❑ | 1 | Back top rail | $^3/_4$ | $3^1/_2$ | $14^7/_8$ | QSWO | $1^1/_4$" TBE |
| ❑ | 1 | Back bottom rail | $^3/_4$ | $4^1/_2$ | $14^7/_8$ | QSWO | $1^1/_4$" TBE |
| ❑ | 1 | Back panel | $^1/_4$ | $11^1/_4$ | $32^7/_8$ | QSWO | |

*Quartersawn white oak; **Tenon both ends; ***Tenon one end*

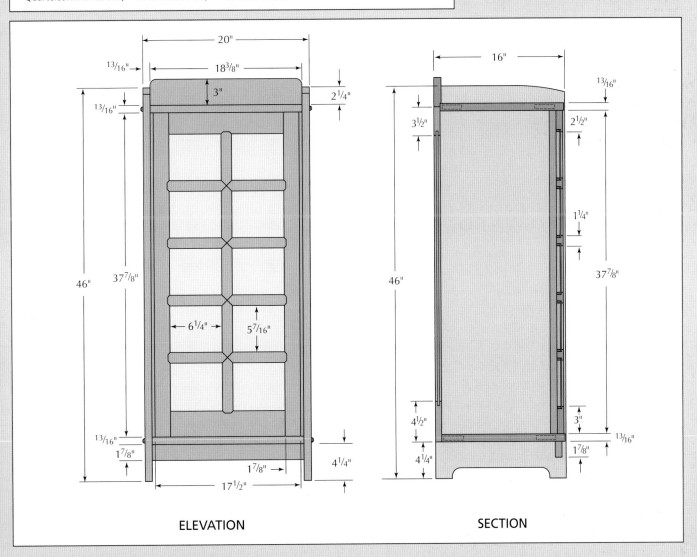

**ELEVATION**

**SECTION**

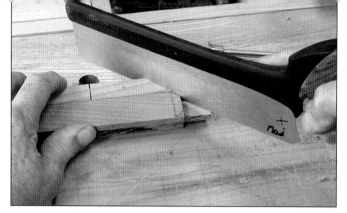

Complex geometry. Test the fit often while fitting the miters. Trimming one edge will lengthen or shorten an adjacent edge as well.

Miters, too. 45° cuts in the fence guide the saw to cut the short miters. Preserve the line at this point, and work down to it while fitting.

Sequence is everything. The parts of the door need to be assembled in order. Do yourself a favor by making a dry run, then use a slow-setting glue.

## A Sharp Edge and a Built-in Guide

The first trick is to use a chisel that is as sharp as you can make it. The end grain of quartersawn white oak will mock you if you try to pare it with anything less than a keen edge, and it will wear that edge quickly. Keep your stones handy; you'll need to hone a few times before you're through.

Angle the chisel so that the flat of the chisel rests against the long, flat edge of the mortise. From that position, simply rotate the business end of the chisel into the corner while keeping the chisel tight against the mortise edge. Get your shoulder over the chisel, and use your body weight as you bring the chisel to vertical.

After a clean line is established in the corner, back the chisel away from the corner and press down, or give it a good smack with a mallet. The short, long-grain edges are easier to pare. Place the edge of the chisel in the knife line made during layout. A push or a tap will do it.

If your chisel work is less than perfect, a small joinery float can be used to refine the corner. Other than the corners, the mortises should be in good shape, thanks to the router and the template. It is important to leave a clean, square edge on the show side. What goes on behind that can remain a secret, and the joint will be strong.

## Tenon Time

To make sure the through-joints look good, I wait until I'm done with the mortises before I start on the tenons. The mortises may grow a little as they are worked, but no one will ever know as long as the tenons fit. I place the board to be tenoned on end, and mark the cuts directly from the mortises.

I cut the shoulder and get a close fit in thickness before worrying about the width of the tenons. I knife in the shoulder line, and clamp a straightedge on the line. With a top-bearing bit in the router, I can sneak up on the right size. I make the first cuts thicker than needed, then measure both the tenon and the mortise with dial calipers.

I then lower the bit by a little less than half the difference of the

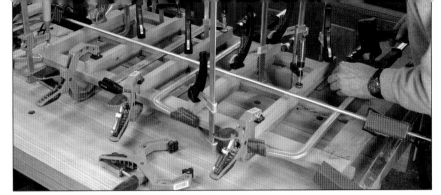

Payday. Flush the surfaces of the completed joints with a sharp block plane, and take a moment to feel proud. Then get back to work; there are a bunch of these.

You need more clamps. The mitered lap joints in the center of the assembly will tend to pop up as clamp pressure is applied to the ends. Battens across the faces hold things together.

Build, don't cut. Assemble small pieces around the layout lines, then use a router with a flush-trim bit to make the mortising template.

16"
6"
2⅜"
2¼"
¾"
½"
2⅜"
1¼"
1¼"
½"
4½"
1¼"
1"
2"  1"
1"  2"

TEMPLATE

measurements and check the fit by placing a corner in the mortise. When the corner can be placed in the mortise I stop. The tenon will be too tight at this point, but it will be close to fitting. The last little bit of thickness will be removed with a float in the next step.

The tenons can be cut at the table saw, but that introduces some risk, and it can be awkward to hold the work on end against a miter gauge or crosscut sled. Cutting the tenons by hand is as fast and accurate. After double-checking the layout and marking with a knife, I cut the long edges of the tenons, and the two outside edges by hand.

And swing it. Keep the back of the chisel pressed against the routed edge of the mortise and carefully rotate the edge into the corner.

The waste in between the two tenons is another story. I cut most of it away with a jigsaw, then clamped a straightedge along the shoulder. With the straightedge in place, I cut a clean edge at the shoulder line with a flush-trim bit in the router.

Before testing the fit, I cut a slight chamfer around the inside edge of the mortise, and around the outermost end of the tenon. This helps to get the tenons started for fitting, and keeps the tenon from chipping out the grain on the outside of the mortise.

Fitting these joints is a bit like detective work. In theory, they should fit at this point, but in reality there will be a bit of wood somewhere that keeps the joint from going home. When the joint sticks, these points need to be found and removed. If you guess and remove material in the wrong place, the result will be a gap in the finished joint.

## Fit Without a Conniption Fit

I push the tenons in as far as I can, then tap on the end of the board a couple times with a dead-blow mallet. When I was younger and my eyes were better, I could see the shiny spots on the tenon where the joint is too tight. These days, I pull out a pencil and draw cross-hatched lines on the tenon and try the fit again. The graphite smears where the joint rubs, showing the high spots. These can be removed with a shoulder plane, but

*Above it all. Line up your shoulder over your hands so you can use your body weight to increase leverage as you pare the end grain.*

*Under control. Cut the tenon shoulders first, using a straightedge and a bearing-guided router bit. Adjust the depth of cut in small increments to achieve the proper thickness.*

it's easy to tilt or go too far. A float is almost as fast, and allows more controlled removal.

As the size of the tenon gets closer to the size of the mortise, I slow down and remove material carefully. The difference between a joint that almost goes together and one that is sloppy can be a matter of a stroke or two.

When I'm satisfied with the fit, I run a pencil around the outer edge of the joint, marking where the tenon pokes through the cabinet side. Then I use a rasp to bevel the ends of the tenons, stopping the bevel about 1/16" from the line. Before assembly, I plane and/or finish-sand the cabinet parts.

It's likely that I will need to refine the surfaces once more after assembly, but the areas around the mortises are difficult to work. This is a point where the desire to see an assembled box tries to take over, but it pays to wait. After sanding, I brush glue inside the mortises and on the end of the

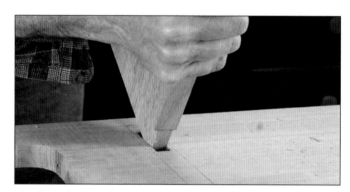

*First things first. Test the thickness of the tenon by placing a corner of the shelf in the mortise. Aim for a tight fit at this point.*

shelves, and let it wick in for about 10 minutes. Then I put glue on the tenons and assemble the carcase.

After clamping, I remove any excess glue and check for square. I've never liked measuring diagonals, so I place corner clamps or square blocks and check each corner with a reliable square. Then I let the assembly dry overnight.

## Details at the End

In most furniture the front is in a single plane, and visual interest comes from applied mouldings. Craftsman furniture does without the trim, and the front of the case is enhanced by setting each element back from its neighbor. The top and bottom are 1/8" back from the sides, the hinges strips are 1/16" in from the top, and the door is back another 1/16".

The hinge stiles sit inside the door opening, and are 1 1/2" wide with a 7/8" deep rabbet, leaving a 3/8" wide edge beside the door. The rabbet acts as a door stop and keeps dust out of the cabinet. After shaping the strip and fixing the hinges I glued these strips to the cabinet sides.

The back is a simple frame and panel. In original examples of this cabinet, the panel was plywood in a solid-wood frame, but I made a 1/4"-thick solid-wood panel. I made the stiles and rails wide so that I could use a single panel from the available material. The bottom front rail is glued to the cabinet bottom.

*Make your mark. Wait until the mortises are completed to lay out the tenons on the cabinet top and bottom. Mark the locations from existing edges.*

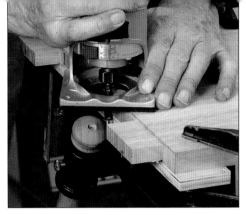

Begin at the end. Cut the ends of the tenons first with a backsaw, then use the same saw to cut away the outside corners.

This will work. Remove the bulk of the waste between the tenons with a jigsaw or coping saw. Then clamp a straightedge between the two tenons and use a router to make a clean, straight cut.

Refined detail. Make a slight bevel on the ends of the tenons before fitting. After a good dry-fit, mark the outside of the case on the tenon, then increase the bevels to end close to the line.

The backsplash is ⅛" thicker than the back panel, with a rabbet on the lower edge to fit over the edge of the cabinet top. This is glued to the edge of the top and at the ends to the sides of the cabinet.

A ¼"-diameter dowel is driven into a hole centered on the front edge of the cabinet side, and the front through tenons. I made the dowels by driving split scraps through a steel dowel plate. The dowels are long enough to reach 1" or so into the edge of the tenons.

This reinforces an overbuilt joint, but it was a feature of the original cabinet, and it looks good after the dowels have been trimmed flush to the front edge. There are four shelves that sit on pins, located so that the shelves fall behind the door muntins.

Our local stained glass shop had textured amber glass for the door, a close match to the original. The glass is held in place with ¼" x ⁷⁄₁₆" strips of wood, mitered and pinned to the inside of the rabbets. The door pull is a close copy of the original, and ball-tipped hinges also are typical. A brass ball catch keeps the door closed.

## No Fume, No Fuss, No-pop Finish

Don't make the mistake of thinking that the finish should make the quartersawn oak "pop." If that's what you're after, use a pigment stain and just about any clear topcoat. The flakes won't take the stain evenly and will be quite evident when you're done.

Original finishes were more subdued – the product of fuming the raw wood with ammonia, and coating with shellac followed by a dark wax. In later years, Craftsman pieces were finished with early versions of modern dye stains and lacquers.

Fuming is an interesting process, but it can be unpredictable and time-consuming. Nearly the same look can be achieved with aniline dye. I stained this piece with Lockwood "#94 Fumed Oak" alcohol-soluble aniline dye. You get a good idea of the final color while the dye is wet; when it dries it looks like you made a terrible mistake.

I follow the dye with a coat of Watco Dark Walnut Danish oil. The oil will add some darker color to the open pores of the wood, act as a glaze to even out the tone and seal the surface. After letting the oil soak in for about 15 minutes, I wiped off the excess and let the surface dry overnight.

The oil over the dye creates a nice chocolate brown color, but the finish needs to be warmed up a bit. A thin coat of amber shellac applied with a rag adds that, and provides some surface protection. I follow the shellac with wax after giving it a couple weeks to fully cure. If the color needs to be toned down or evened out, a dark wax can be used instead of clear.

Overkill. The dowel reinforces the through mortise and tenon joint. It isn't needed, but its a nice detail to include.

Layered look. Aniline dye stain is coated with tinted Danish oil. This will be followed by a thin coat of amber shellac.

# Jig for Through Mortise

A jig is, by definition, a problem-solving device. As such, it shouldn't take more time to make the jig than it would to perform the operation without it. If the purpose of the jig is to replace an operation that requires a lot of skill, how can you make the jig if you lack the skills? There is no shortage of published jigs that fail miserably on the above points. I think there may be woodworkers out there whose hobby is limited to building jigs, but for the rest of us, here is a simple method for making a jig to cut a square hole. In this case, I'm making the through-mortises in the case sides of a Stickley music cabinet.

I cut a piece of ½"-thick plywood to the width of the case side, and long enough to include the through-mortises at the top and bottom, as well as the shape of a cutout at the bottom (the pencil lines at the left) and a rounded drop at the front of the cabinet (the pencil lines at the right). I also cut some strips a couple inches wide to support the router, and some ½" wide, which is the width of the finished mortise. You can see my layout lines for the mortises on the right side.

I've taken some double-sides tape, and covered the layout lines so I can stick the small plywood pieces to the large piece. The quality of double-sides tape can vary, I like to use Speed Tape which is strong enough to be a permanent adhesive. I place the plywood strips around the layout lines for the mortises. This is easy to do and it saves me from cutting a square hole in the plywood.

When I'm finished, I take a dead-blow hammer and tap on the strips to set the adhesive on the tape. Now I'm ready to take a router with a flush-trimming bit and make the cut outs for the mortises, after I drill a ⅜"-diameter hole in the middle of each opening that allows the router bit to pass through.

I put some blocks on top of my bench, flip the plywood over and proceed to rout the openings. The bearing on the bit follows the little pieces of plywood and makes the cut right on my layout lines. The bit leaves the corners rounded, but I've accomplished my goal; I have nice straight edges that are square to each other and the exact size I want.

I don't need the strips anymore, so I pop them off. There are circumstances where I might want to have the jig a full 1" thick. In that case I would hold the strips down with yellow glue and leave them on permanently. The extra thickness can help guide a chisel for squaring the corners. I don't care for that method, even though it makes a good chiseling jig. The downside is you can't see inside on a narrow mortise and you have to chisel the corners of the plywood square.

I just leave the corners of the jig round. I lay out the mortise locations on the solid-wood case side, and mark them with a knife. The knife cuts will guide my chisel when I trim, and prevent the router bit from tearing out around the line. This jig was quick to make, I didn't have to do a lot of fussy cutting to make it, and it allowed me to make eight through-mortises in a short period of time. Here is the end result:

# ▶ Refinforcing the Indestrucible

Pegging through-mortise-and-tenon joints is an excellent way to reinforce the already strong joint.

Good dowels can be hard (if not impossible) to find, so when I need the right size and the right species, I make my own. It doesn't take long, and the work is a nice relief from fussing with other details. I start with a straight-grained piece of scrap about 3" long, and split off pieces with a chisel. All it takes is a good rap with a mallet after I put the chisel in place.

I start by aiming for about ⅜"-square blanks to make ¼" dowels. Sometimes the split will be off course, and the blank is made smaller by laying it down on the bench and continuing the splitting by placing a wide chisel on the wood and pressing down or tapping with a mallet. Essentially, this is riving lumber on a small scale. It doesn't take long to get the hang of it, and it doesn't matter if I lose a few in the process. Split material works much better than sawn for making these short lengths. The blank is stronger because the grain is continuous throughout the length.

When the blanks are close to the right size, I knock the corners off with the chisel or by whittling with a knife. I whittle down the end to make it easier to start in the holes in the dowel plate. The plate is just a ¼"-thick piece of scrap steel with a series of holes drilled in it. The holes are in steps of ¹⁄₁₆" and I didn't bother trying to sharpen them. If they get dull I may take a flat file across the face to create a burr, but this works just fine. If that's too simple for you, you can buy a fancy dowel plate or try to harden and hone the thing. To use it, I start with a large hole and pound the blank through. The

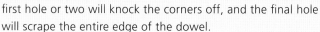

first hole or two will knock the corners off, and the final hole will scrape the entire edge of the dowel.

With a brad-point drill, I drill through the front edge and about 1" into the tenon. I put a dab of glue in the hole, and drive the dowel in place. After the glue dries, I trim it flush with a saw, then pare it down flush with a chisel. A few swipes with a block plane and it's finished.

That's the how to do it part. But why go to that much trouble to reinforce a joint like that – where is it going to go?

I confess that I don't have a good answer, except that I was copying an original detail that does make a statement about building for forever. But here's how I usually explain it, "It's just in case there's a disturbance in the earth's magnetic field that yanks us out of orbit and sends us toward the sun. On the way to oblivion it might get hot enough for all the glue to melt and for the wood to shrink enough to pull out. Other than that, I don't think you need to do it."

# ▶ When A&C Joinery Becomes Decoration

A large part of the appeal of Arts and Crafts style furniture is the apparent lack of decoration. This project, a reproduction of a Gustav Stickley No. 70 music cabinet and a detail I've borrowed from similar pieces is the reason for using the word "apparent". I've always liked this little cabinet, it's just under four feet high, and only 20 inches wide. The detail I borrowed, mitered mullions on the door, and the idea of plain, unadorned furniture is hard to reconcile. As I worked on the door, I came to realize that there isn't any practical reason to put a glass door on a cabinet to store sheet music, and joining the parts of the door this way is just showing off.

I've always liked this detail where the cross pieces that divide the door join the center stile with what appear to be simple miters, and it was an intriguing challenge to figure out how it was done and then to execute the joinery. I found three variations of joints on the other end, and decided to take a middle of the road approach. Some pieces I've seen are straightforward mortise and tenon joints where the mullions butt against the stiles, others have a reflection of the center stile joints, and some are made as shown above with the miter going back to the edge of the rabbet that holds the glass. I didn't like the way a full miter would encroach on the tenon, and I thought the butted shoulders looked too plain.

In an earlier blog post I wrote about making a practice joint, and I used the strategy I came up with; cutting the miter lines with a backsaw, using a router and jig to create a flat area within the cutout, and finally cleaning up the corners with a chisel. The center door stile became more and more valuable as I cut and fit each joint, there are a lot of hours in that skinny piece of wood.

This is one of the joints ready to be glued, it looks a lot simpler when it's together, but the lap joints keep the pieces from sliding around and the shoulders behind make it strong structurally, even though it is end grain butting against long grain. There really isn't room in there for anything else. It took a boatload of clamps to hold it all together, but the glue up wasn't that bad and the completed door is pretty strong. As my boss put it "you'd have to shove somebody's head right into it to bust it."

And here is the door after a night in the clamps, as I clean up the surfaces. I'm working on the cabinet now, but it feels like coasting even though there are eight through mortises in the carcase. So far, everyone who has seen this door has had the same two stage reaction, myself included. Part one is "wow that must have been a lot of work". Part two is "but it looks incredibly cool". That makes it all worthwhile.

# Arts & Crafts Bridal Chest

## Contrasting woods highlight the elegant lines of this Gustav Stickley-designed classic.

In days gone by, a chest similar to this would contain a bride's dowry. The form goes back to Gothic times, but this is an adaptation of a Gustav Stickley piece from 1901. Admiring the lines of this piece, I was curious to see how the design would look with contrasting materials, not the usual Craftsman dark oak. The panels are quilted bird's eye maple, and the other parts are Jatoba, also known as Brazilian cherry.

The original was made of quartersawn white oak with wrought-iron braces on the corners. What makes this unusual for a Stickley design are the decorative corbels on the panels. These also appeared on a few dining room case pieces made in the early 1900s.

Decorative curved elements in Stickley furniture are usually associated with Harvey Ellis, who worked for Stickley in 1903. This design appeared well before Ellis worked for Stickley, and before Stickley wrote against using purely decorative elements in his furniture catalogs.

Stickley doesn't always get the credit he deserves as a furniture designer. Building this bridal chest with non-traditional materials takes his design out of the Craftsman context, and shows Stickley's remarkable sense of line, proportion and texture.

In many of the original bridal chests I have seen, the center panels have cracked. I think the corbels are the culprits, keeping the solid-wood panels from expanding and contracting in the grooves of the stiles. To avoid this problem, I decided to use veneered panels. The veneer is on a core of ½"-thick Medium-density Fiberboard (MDF), and the backing veneer is sycamore, a less-expensive alternative to the figured faces.

The veneer on the wider center and end panels is book-matched. I pressed the panels one at a time in a simple shop-made cold press, and worked on the chest's solid-wood components while the glue on the panels was curing.

If you think of this chest as a simple box, most of the work is in the five paneled assemblies: the front and back, two ends and the top. The panel assemblies are joined with mortises and tenons, and each of the four legs is really two stiles with the long edges mitered together.

I fabricated all of the stiles and rails, and then dry-fit each of the panel assemblies before cutting and assembling the miter joints that connect the legs.

## Managing Bits and Pieces

This isn't really a difficult project to build; the hardest part is keeping track of what piece goes where. The applied corbels make it necessary for the panel grooves to be off-center on the edges of the stiles and rails. As I cut the parts I decided where they would go in the finished chest, and marked each one with a lumber crayon. As I worked on the joints I paid close attention to which face of each part was the outside piece.

After cutting the panel parts to size, I grouped four of the leg pieces together and marked them out as left-handed

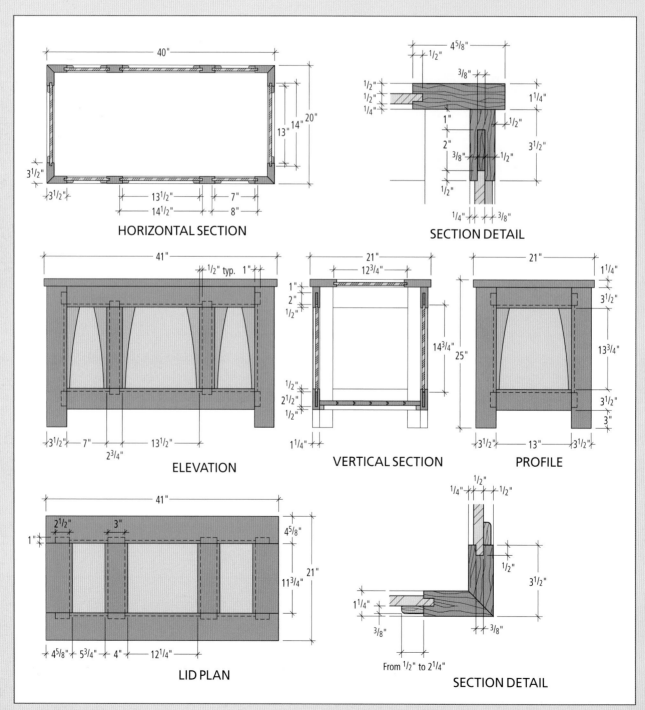

HORIZONTAL SECTION

SECTION DETAIL

ELEVATION

VERTICAL SECTION

PROFILE

LID PLAN

SECTION DETAIL

pieces, using a story pole to transfer the measurements. I then laid out the other four leg pieces as right-handed, marking the locations of the grooves for the panels and the mortises that hold the stiles and rails together.

The mortises are the same width as, and in line with, the grooves that capture the panels. These ³⁄₈"-wide grooves are set ¹⁄₂" back from the outside face of the stiles and rails, so I had to be careful to keep all the parts oriented correctly as I milled the grooves.

I cut the stopped grooves with a stack dado set on the table saw, carefully lowering and raising the legs on and off the cutters. Because the mortises fall in the ends of the grooves, the exact length of the grooves isn't critical. The grooves in the rails and in the intermediate stiles run the full length of those parts. After milling all the grooves, I began making mortises with my hollow-chisel mortiser, setting the distance from the fence to the chisel to match the location of the groove.

The tenons were cut with a stack dado set on the table saw, and then trimmed to a piston fit with a shoulder plane. With the individual panels dry-assembled, I made sure that the faces of the joints were flush with a few swipes of my smoothing plane.

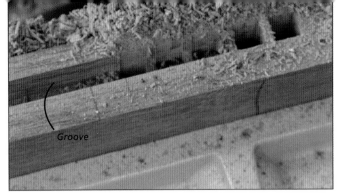

*The mortiser is set with the chisel flush with the panel groove. Plunge the bit and chisel to make distinct holes, then come back and clean up the waste in between.*

*With the dimensions marked on a story pole, the locations for the mortises are marked on the legs as a group.*

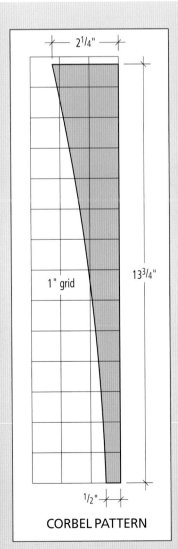

2¹⁄₄"

1" grid

13³⁄₄"

¹⁄₂"

**CORBEL PATTERN**

## Arts & crafts bridal chest

| NO. | ITEM | DIMENSIONS (INCHES) T | W | L | MATERIAL | COMMENTS |
|---|---|---|---|---|---|---|
| ❑ 2 | Top stiles | 1¹⁄₄ | 4⁵⁄₈ | 41 | Jatoba | |
| ❑ 2 | Top end rails | 1¹⁄₄ | 4⁵⁄₈ | 13³⁄₄ | Jatoba | 11³⁄₄" between tenons, 1" TBE |
| ❑ 2 | Top center rails | 1¹⁄₄ | 4 | 13³⁄₄ | Jatoba | 11³⁄₄" between tenons, 1" TBE |
| ❑ 2 | Top end panels | ¹⁄₂ | 6³⁄₄ | 12³⁄₄ | Maple | ³⁄₈" x ¹⁄₂" tongue around edge |
| ❑ 1 | Top center panel | ¹⁄₂ | 13¹⁄₄ | 12³⁄₄ | Maple | ³⁄₈" x ¹⁄₂" tongue around edge |
| ❑ 8 | Legs | 1¹⁄₄ | 3¹⁄₂ | 23³⁄₄ | Jatoba | |
| ❑ 4 | F&B, top & bottom rails | 1¹⁄₄ | 3¹⁄₂ | 35 | Jatoba | 33" between tenons, 1" TBE |
| ❑ 4 | F&B, center stiles | 1¹⁄₄ | 2³⁄₄ | 15³⁄₄ | Jatoba | 13³⁄₄" between tenons, 1" TBE |
| ❑ 4 | F&B end panels | ¹⁄₂ | 8 | 14³⁄₄ | Maple | ³⁄₈" x ¹⁄₂" tongue around edge |
| ❑ 2 | F&B center panels | ¹⁄₂ | 14¹⁄₂ | 14³⁄₄ | Maple | ³⁄₈" x ¹⁄₂" tongue around edge |
| ❑ 4 | Side, top & bottom rails | 1¹⁄₄ | 3¹⁄₂ | 15 | Jatoba | 13" between tenons, 1" TBE |
| ❑ 2 | Side panels | ¹⁄₂ | 14 | 14³⁄₄ | Maple | ³⁄₈" x ¹⁄₂" tongue around edge |
| ❑ 16 | Corbels | ³⁄₈ | 2¹⁄₄ | 13³⁄₄ | Jatoba | Cut to pattern |
| ❑ 2 | Bottom cleats | ³⁄₄ | ³⁄₄ | 37¹⁄₂ | Jatoba | |
| ❑ 2 | Bottom cleats | ³⁄₄ | ³⁄₄ | 16 | Jatoba | |
| ❑ 5 | Bottom planks | ³⁄₄ | 3³⁄₁₆ | 37¹⁄₂ | Cedar | ¹⁄₄" x ¹⁄₄" tongue & groove |
| ❑ 1 | Bottom plank | ³⁄₄ | 2¹⁵⁄₁₆ | 37¹⁄₂ | Cedar | ¹⁄₄" x ¹⁄₄" groove |

*TBE: Tenon both ends*

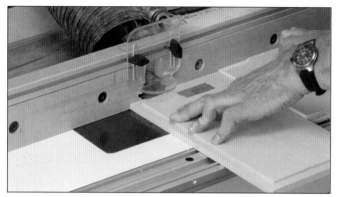

*Each of the tenons is planed to fit snugly in its mortise. A batten across the bench eliminates the need to clamp the parts while fitting.*

Batten

*Setting the cutter above the table surface cuts a consistently sized tongue on the back of the panels.*

## Getting Ready to Assemble

I cut the veneered panels to their final size, and then milled a rabbet on the back of each panel on the router table. With a slot-cutting bit set just under 3/8" above the table surface, I made a tongue that slipped in the grooves of the stiles and rails. This is a good technique when working with plywood panels of inconsistent thickness as the fixed distance between the table and cutter will produce a consistent part that matches the width of the groove. I then sanded the veneered panels to #220 grit to prepare things for assembly.

Before assembling any of the panels, I cut 45° bevels on the long edge of each leg that didn't have the groove for the panels. I glued pairs of legs together, clamping them with a combination of clear packing tape and clamps. After letting the glue on these joints dry overnight, I glued together the front- and back-panel assemblies. The two end-panel assemblies are put together as the entire case is assembled. With the back panel lying face down on the bench, I assembled the rails and panels for the sides. Once they were in place, I put glue on the tenons and dropped the front panel assembly in place. I then set the chest upright on my bench and clamped across the ends, checking for square.

After the glue on the solid parts had dried, I sanded the outside of the chest with a random-orbit sander, working from #100 grit up to #220, followed by a hand sanding with #280 grit. The top panel was then put together and sanded smooth.

## Adding the Corbels

I made the 3/8"-thick corbels by resawing some of the 1 1/4"-thick stock left over from making the rest of the chest. After planing them to thickness, I stacked four pieces together with double-faced carpet tape holding the layers together. I made a pattern of the corbel shape from 1/2" MDF, and traced the outline on the top layer of the stack.

*Strips of clear packing tape across the joint let the miters fold together. More tape and additional clamps provide a tight, strong joint.*

*Rails and panels for the sides are slipped into the already-assembled back panel.*

Using stock a few inches longer than I needed, and interlocking the patterns, I was able to get eight corbels from each stack. I cut the pieces on the band saw, and sanded the curved edges on the spindle sander before taking the stacks apart. With a 1/8"-radius roundover bit in my laminate trimmer, I eased the curved edges before sanding the corbels.

The corbels are glued to the panels and edges of the stiles. I used a couple 3/4"-long 23-gauge headless pins to fasten the wider part of the corbels to the panels, filling the nail holes with some sawdust and cyanoacrylate glue. I hand sanded the entire cabinet, and applied three coats of Waterlox wiping varnish before hinging the lid and putting in the tongue-and-groove bottom.

I used four 2½"-long, no-mortise hinges for the lid, spacing them evenly along the top rail of the back of the chest. To hold the lid in the open position, I used a pair of toy-box supports. Because the chest was still bottomless, I could lay it on its back on my bench, and reach inside to position the supports.

## Getting to the Bottom

I don't have a daughter, so this chest will live at the foot of our bed, holding extra blankets. I placed 3/4" by 3/4" cleats around the perimeter of the bottom, flush with the bottom edge of the rails. The bottom planks are 3/4"-thick aromatic cedar, held together with simple tongue-and-groove joints. I nailed the bottom planks to the cleats at the edges and ends. The cedar is left unfinished.

In the end, this chest has a clean, contemporary look with classic proportions. Changing the material may have disguised its origin, but the strength of the design shines through. Good design, after all, is timeless.

## Supplies

**Rockler**
800-279-4441 | rockler.com

2 pair ▶ bronze no-mortise hinges
  #28696, $3.99/pair

1 ▶ RH lid support
  #26229, $10.29

1 ▶ LH lid support
  #26195, $10.29

*Assembling the front and back panels first simplifies the final assembly – putting the sides together results in a completed case.*

*The assembled chest is flipped upright, the corners are checked for square and the case is clamped.*

*A stack of four blanks held together with double-sided tape yields eight matching corbels.*

*The difference in thickness between the corbel and the adjacent stile and rail adds visual interest.*

*After cutting, the edges are sanded with the stack still stuck together.*

# Byrdcliffe Linen Press

## Recreating a classic cabinet that breaks the rules of Arts & Crafts.

The history of most pieces of furniture can be traced back to one individual – usually the designer, the maker or the client. The roots of this linen press spread to include a fascinating group of people at an early 20th-century art colony known as Byrdcliffe, located near Woodstock, N.Y.

With its carved door panels and distinctive colors, this unusual cabinet is one of the finest examples of the Arts & Crafts period. The basic form can be traced back to English designs of the period, but the stylized carving and overall proportions make it unique. The original is part of the collection of the Metropolitan Museum of Art in New York.

Fewer than 50 pieces of furniture were made at Byrdcliffe between 1903 and 1905. Fewer than half of those found buyers; the remaining pieces were found in various buildings at the colony after the 1976 death of the founder's son. Many of these had been left unfinished, the idea being that the buyer could choose a color when purchasing.

# Byrdcliffe linen press

| NO. | ITEM | T | W | L | MATERIAL | COMMENTS |
|---|---|---|---|---|---|---|
| **CARCASE** | | | | | | |
| 8 | Leg front & back | 1 | 2½ | 54¼ | Quartersawn white oak | Miter long edges |
| 8 | Leg sides | 1⅛ | 2½ | 54¼ | Quartersawn white oak | Miter & rabbet long edges |
| 4 | Side panel stiles | ¾ | 3½ | 44½ | Quartersawn white oak | |
| 2 | Side panel top rails | ¾ | 6½ | 8⅜ | Quartersawn white oak | 1¼" TBE |
| 2 | Side panel middle rails | ¾ | 5⅛ | 8⅜ | Quartersawn white oak | 1¼" TBE |
| 2 | Side panel bottom rails | ¾ | 3⅝ | 8⅜ | Quartersawn white oak | 1¼" TBE |
| 2 | Lower arched rails | ⅞ | 5⅛ | 8⅜ | Quartersawn white oak | 1¼" TBE |
| 2 | Top side panels | ⅝ | 6⅞ | 13 | Quartersawn white oak | ½" TAS |
| 2 | Bottom side panels | ⅝ | 6⅞ | 18¼ | Quartersawn white oak | ½" TAS |
| 1 | Top | ¾ | 18¾ | 41 | Quartersawn white oak | |
| 1 | Front top rail | ⅞ | 2⅝ | 34¾ | Quartersawn white oak | 1" TBE |
| 2 | Drawer rails | ⅞ | 1¼ | 34¾ | Quartersawn white oak | 1" TBE |
| 1 | Bottom front rail | ⅞ | 1⅜ | 34¾ | Quartersawn white oak | 1" TBE |
| 1 | Bottom apron | ¾ | 6¾ | 34¾ | Quartersawn white oak | 1" TBE |
| 2 | Stiles @ doors | ¾ | 2³⁄₁₆ | 19¾ | Quartersawn white oak | |
| 2 | Stiles @ top drawer | ¾ | 2³⁄₁₆ | 7½ | Quartersawn white oak | |
| 2 | Stiles @ bottom drawer | ¾ | 2³⁄₁₆ | 8½ | Quartersawn white oak | |
| 1 | Drawer rail support | ¾ | 1⅜ | 32¾ | Quartersawn white oak | |
| 2 | Fill behind crown | ⅜ | 1⁵⁄₁₆ | 12⅛ | Quartersawn white oak | |
| 1 | Fill behind crown | ¼ | 1⁵⁄₁₆ | 32¾ | Quartersawn white oak | |
| 6 | Web frame stiles | ¾ | 2½ | 35½ | Poplar | |
| 9 | Web frame rails | ¾ | 2½ | 10⅞ | Poplar | ¾" TBE |
| 4 | Web frame panels | ¾ | 10⅜ | 14¾ | Plywood | |
| 2 | Crown moulding | 1 | 2 | 48 | Quartersawn white oak | |
| **DOORS** | | | | | | |
| 2 | Door hinge stiles | ¾ | 3⅞ | 19¾ | Quartersawn white oak | |
| 1 | Left lock stile | ¾ | 3⅞ | 19¾ | Quartersawn white oak | |
| 1 | Right lock stile | ¾ | 4⅛ | 19¾ | Quartersawn white oak | |
| 2 | Door top rails | ¾ | 3⅞ | 9¾ | Quartersawn white oak | 1" TBE |
| 2 | Door bottom rails | ¾ | 3⅞ | 9¾ | Quartersawn white oak | 1" TBE |
| 2 | Door panels | ⅝ | 8¾ | 13 | Basswood | ½" TAS |
| **DRAWERS** | | | | | | |
| 1 | Top drawer front | ¾ | 7½ | 31¼ | Quartersawn white oak | Opening size trim to fit |
| 1 | Bottom drawer front | ¾ | 8½ | 31¼ | Quartersawn white oak | Opening size trim to fit |
| 2 | Drawer sides | ¾ | 7½ | 14¼ | Maple | Dovetailed to front |
| 2 | Drawer sides | ¾ | 8½ | 14¼ | Maple | Dovetailed to front |
| 1 | Drawer back | ¾ | 7½ | 32¾ | Maple | In dado in sides |
| 1 | Drawer back | ¾ | 8½ | 32¾ | Maple | In dado in sides |
| 2 | Drawer bottoms | ¼ | 14½ | 30⅜ | Plywood | |
| 4 | Drawer runners | 1 | 1½ | 14¼ | Quartersawn white oak | ¾" TOE |
| **BACK** | | | | | | |
| 3 | Back frame rails | ¾ | 2½ | 30 | Poplar | ¾" TBE |
| 3 | Back frame stiles | ¾ | 2½ | 43⅜ | Poplar | |
| 2 | Back planks | ½ | 4⅞ | 43⅜ | Poplar | ¼" rabbet one edge |
| 4 | Back planks | ½ | 4⅞ | 43⅜ | Poplar | ¼ " rabbet both edges |

*TBE = Tenon Both Ends; TAS= Tenon All Sides; TOE= Tenon One End*

## The Cast of Characters

Byrdcliffe was founded and financed by Englishman Ralph Radcliffe Whitehead. He inherited the family's felt fortune at age 32, and was a follower of John Ruskin. Although not an artistic man himself, he married a painter, and enjoyed the company of many prominent artists and intellectuals.

In the early 1890s, he wrote about an idealized community of artists, but didn't act on these plans until the birth of his two sons gave him a desire to do something useful with his fortune. He purchased 1,300 acres of land, built about 30 buildings, including a well-equipped woodshop and surrounded himself with a talented group of artists and writers.

Although Whitehead held artists in high esteem, he had a rather low opinion of craftsmen. In his written plan for his community he stated: "Now, in order to have anything good made in stuff, or in hard material, we must seek out the artist to provide us with a design, and then a workman to carry it out as mechanically as possible, because we know that if he puts any of his coarser self into it he will spoil it."

Who actually made and carved the furniture produced at Byrdcliffe is not known. Apparently there were several different cabinetmakers, as the quality of construction varies from piece to piece. Although Byrdcliffe was intended to be self-supporting, Whitehead was wealthy enough to abandon the furniture-making part of his plan after a little more

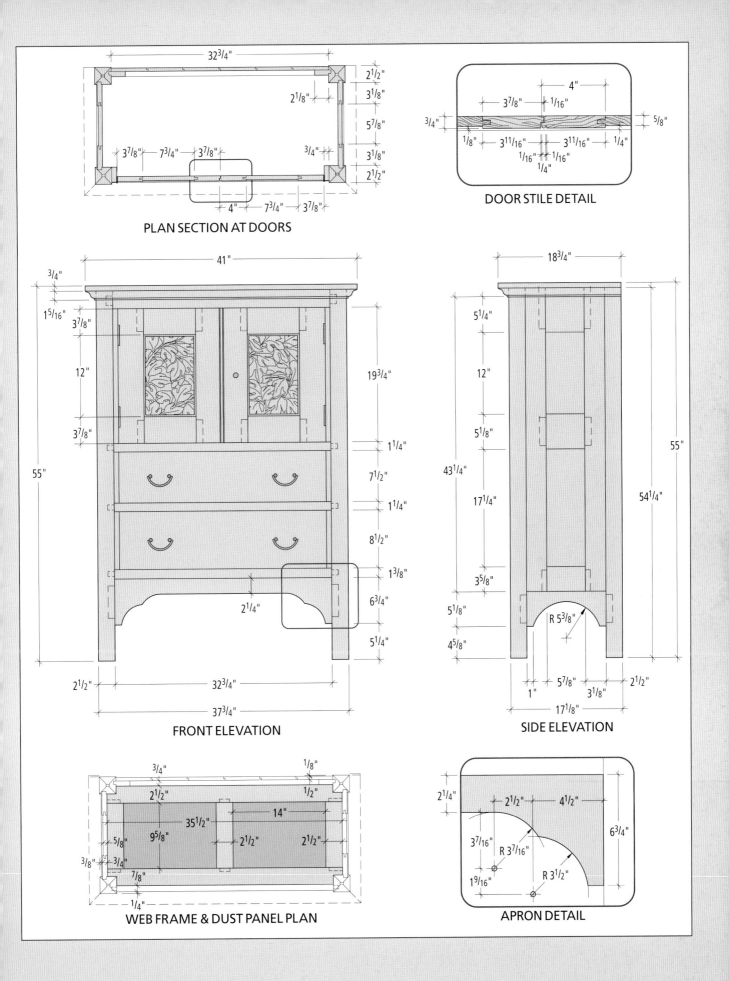

PLAN SECTION AT DOORS

DOOR STILE DETAIL

FRONT ELEVATION

SIDE ELEVATION

WEB FRAME & DUST PANEL PLAN

APRON DETAIL

than a year of dealing with the "coarser" workmen.

Many of the artists in residence created furniture designs. Apparently Whitehead selected a general form, and drawings were made by individual artists. Decorative panels were a common feature, although most were painted, not carved. Among the most talented designers at Byrdcliffe were Edna Walker and Zulma Steele. This piece was designed by Walker.

The designs by Walker and Steele are the most beautifully proportioned and distinctive pieces of Byrdcliffe furniture. This cabinet in particular is a refreshing break from the mass and machismo of many Arts & Crafts pieces.

## 100 Years Later

Usually when I make a reproduction of an existing piece I try to stay as close as possible to the original. In building this cabinet, however, I had to make some guesses, and I made a few changes to suit my own taste. I had only a photograph of the front of the cabinet and overall dimensions to work with, so the layout of the side panels and the details of construction are my best guesses.

In the original, the carvings are very flat. They are simply outlines of leaves and branches with the edges rounded over. I originally carved the panels this way, but just wasn't happy with the effect. I thought they seemed rather lifeless and static, so I recarved the panels and added more relief.

Additionally, the crown moulding on the original comes flush to the bottom edge of the top, apparently attached to the edges. The closest router bit I could find (Freud 99-406) had a small fillet at the top. I thought this looked nicer, and rather than wrap the crown around the perimeter of the top, I set it below, letting the top overhang by ⅛". This added one more shadow line, and if the top expands or contracts, then the joint between the moulding and the top won't show.

The third change was to the color. The oranges and reds on the panels are the same as the original, but the green stain is darker and deeper in color. The finish on the original varies in color, and I suspect that it may have faded or been refinished at some point. I decided to use a richer forest green, similar to a color that can be seen in another Byrdcliffe piece, a fall-front desk designed by Steele.

## Oak and (not) Sassafras

Like the original, the visible parts of this cabinet are made of quartersawn white oak. The carved panels are often described as being made from sassafras, but they are obviously not. The carving depicts the leaves of a sassafras tree and in the original the panels are either poplar or basswood. I used basswood for the carvings, soft maple for the drawer boxes, and poplar for the interior web frames and back of the cabinet. The dust

A group of stiles for the web frame is clamped together to lay out the joints. Leaving the stack clamped together provides a stable base for the router used to cut the mortises.

panels are birch plywood.

I brought the rough white oak into the shop and let it acclimate while I worked on carving the panels (right). I'm a decent carver, but not a fast one, so the oak had plenty of time to adjust. Full-size patterns for the panels are available in pdf format from our web site at: *www.popularwoodworking. com/wp-content/uploads/2010/10/iris.pdf.*

I gave the completed panels a thin coat of blonde shellac before coloring them with watercolor pencils, available from any artist's supply store. The colors are applied dry, then blended with an artist's brush dipped in water. I let the panels dry for several days, then gave them two coats of amber shellac to seal in the color and warm up the background.

## The Real Work Begins

I milled all of the oak parts slightly oversized, and let them sit for a few days before planing them to finished dimensions. Absolutely straight stock is essential for a project like this. The side panels are all joined with mortises and tenons. Once these were assembled, I cut a rabbet on the long edge of each panel so that the faces of the stiles fit in a stopped groove cut in the legs as seen at right (page 46). This makes the sides of the case very strong, and if the stiles shrink in width over time, the joints won't open up.

The web frames and dust panels are also mortise-and-tenon construction. I clamped the stiles together to lay out the mortises and then realized that leaving them clamped together

## Doors carved, then colored

After tracing the pattern on the basswood panels, the design of sassafras leaves is carved.

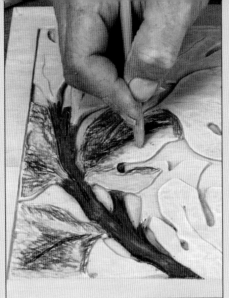

The completed carving is given a wash coat of shellac, then colors are applied with watercolor pencils.

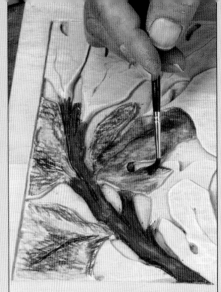

The colors are blended with an artist's brush dipped in water.

After the coloring is complete, the panels are allowed to dry several days before being finished with amber shellac.

would provide a stable base for the small plunge router I used to cut the mortises (above).

## Impossible Legs

Like a lot of Arts & Crafts furniture, the legs are an important element. The problem with quartersawn oak in this situation is two-fold: Thick stock usually isn't available, and the edge grain is ugly compared to the face grain. There are several ways to work around this, and the method I developed shows quartersawn figure on all four faces of the legs, and is relatively simple to mill and assemble.

I could have laminated the legs from thinner stock and then veneered the edges, but I have seen too many old pieces constructed this way that have cracks in the veneer. Quarter-sawn wood moves more in thickness than in width, so there's a good chance that this method will eventually fail.

Mitering four pieces together is a logical alternative, but without some way to keep the pieces from sliding during glue-up, assembly can be very difficult. In the early 1900s, Leopold Stickley developed a method that used rabbeted miters to form what he called a quadralinear leg. It's a good method, but without the custom-made shaper cutters he used it is difficult to mill.

Looking for a simpler method, I realized that by making the front and back pieces of the legs a different thickness than the sides, I could make two of the pieces with simple miters, and use a small rabbet on the thicker pieces to keep the parts from sliding during assembly. The photos on pages 47-48 show the steps I took.

The side panels are assembled as a unit, then fit in a groove in the leg, and butted at the bottom to the thicker arched rail.

The web frames are notched around the legs and attached to the side rails with pocket screws. The front and back edges will be glued to the rails as they are assembled.

Several joints must be fit at one time as the second panel and leg assembly is put in place. Get some help so both sides can be fit and clamped at the same time.

The drawers and drawer fronts are fit before finishing the cabinet. After hanging the doors, I mark where the right door overlaps the left before cutting the rabbet.

When I had the legs assembled, I used a plunge router with a fence to cut the stopped grooves for the side and back panels, then laid out and cut the mortises in the front legs for the rails at the front of the carcase.

The side panel assembly is placed in the groove in the leg, and the arched bottom rail is placed in its mortise. The two pieces are then glued and butted together where they meet before the second leg is put in place. With the left and right leg and panel sides together, the entire carcase can be assembled.

With one side panel and leg asssembly face down on some

horses, I notched the corners of the web frames around the legs, and held them in place with pocket screws. The back frame was then put in the groove in the rear leg, followed by the front rails in their mortises. The butt joints between the rails and the front edge of the frames were glued and clamped at this time, as were the joints between the web frames and the back frame.

Putting the second leg and panel assembly on is straightforward, but there are a lot of parts that need to come precisely together. I made a dry run, and then got some help to fit it all

**1**

After ripping all the parts to finished width, cut a 45° bevel on both long edges of the thinner parts. Cutting the second bevel brings the part to its finished width.

**2**

Be careful ripping the second bevel. After the leading edge clears the blade, use a push stick centered in the stock's width to move the material past the saw blade without tilting it.

**3**

Set up to cut the grooves in the bottom of the thick pieces. With a thin piece of scrap against a thicker one, draw a line to indicate the difference in thickness. Flip the thicker piece over and use the pencil line to set the height of the saw blade.

**4**

Set the distance from the blade to the fence by lining up the edge of a thin piece of stock to the left side of the blade. I use the saw cut in the table saw's zero-clearance insert as a guide.

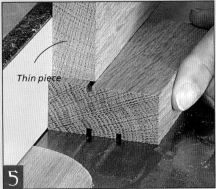

*Thin piece*

**5**

Make some test cuts in scrap. Check the width of the groove by placing the edge of the scrap against the fence, and a thin piece of scrap on top. When the corner of the thin piece meets the far edge of the groove, the fence is set correctly.

*Thin piece*

**6**

Check the depth of the groove by placing a thin piece on the saw table, and butt the thicker piece against it. The face of the thin piece should meet the bottom of the groove.

---

## making the legs

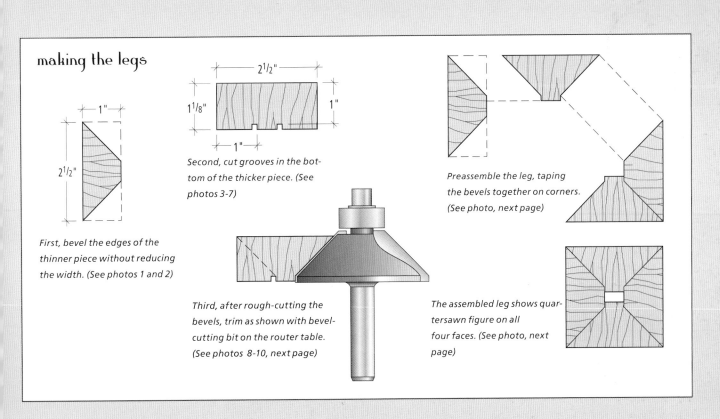

First, bevel the edges of the thinner piece without reducing the width. (See photos 1 and 2)

*2½"* — *1"*

2½"

Second, cut grooves in the bottom of the thicker piece. (See photos 3-7)

2½"
1⅛"
1"
1"

Third, after rough-cutting the bevels, trim as shown with bevel-cutting bit on the router table. (See photos 8-10, next page)

Preassemble the leg, taping the bevels together on corners. (See photo, next page)

The assembled leg shows quartersawn figure on all four faces. (See photo, next page)

▶ CASEWORK **47**

7

With the blade height and fence settings adjusted, cut two grooves in the back of the thicker leg parts.

8

After the grooves are cut, the saw is again tilted to 45° and the waste is removed. Leave about ¹/₄" of flat on the edge to ride against the router table fence.

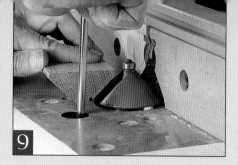

9

The 45° bevel bit is set to intersect the corner of the groove and the edge of the workpiece. The goal is to create the bevel without reducing the width on the face of the piece.

10

After making some test cuts and fine tuning the router table setup, the edges are beveled. The block behind the featherboard holds it away from the fence, so it is pushing down on the narrow flat left between the two bevels.

11

After all the parts are milled, I assemble the corners and hold them together with packing tape. All but the last corner is taped before gluing. I then flip the taped parts over, put glue on the edges, then fold the parts back together, taping the last corner.

12

The completed legs have a small rectangular hollow in the center, and show quartersawn figure on all four sides. This is a stable assembly, relatively quick to make and easy to assemble.

together and apply the clamps.

## Not Done Yet

Usually, getting the carcase assembled means that the end is in sight, but this cabinet contains several details that require additional work. Much of the interest of this design comes from the varying setbacks of the faces of the parts, particularly those on the front elevation.

The side panels are set back ³/₈" from the face of the legs, and the arched rail below it is ¹/₈" thicker. On the front of the cabinet, the rails are back ¹/₄" from the legs. At the top of the cabinet, filler strips were glued on so the back of the crown moulding would be flush with the outside edges of the legs.

The lower front rail and the stiles for the door hinges are ¹/₁₆" back from the rails, as are the vertical pieces beside the drawers.

The hinge stiles allow the doors to swing clear of the legs, and this detail is seen in many pieces of Arts & Crafts furniture. The doors and drawer fronts are ¹/₁₆" back from the front edge of the stiles. On the doors this offset is accomplished when locating the hinges. The placement of the stopped groove in the side of the drawer boxes locates the face of the drawer fronts.

The stiles for the hinges were cut and put in place, and the doors were assembled without glue so that all of the cutting for the hinge mortises could be done conveniently. Once I was satisfied with the fit of the doors, I marked where the right door overlaps the left, took everything apart and then glued the hinge stiles in place.

## Drawer Runners

The drawers are rather wide, so I decided to use wood runners to guide them in and out without the bottoms of the drawer box sides rubbing on the web frames or the front rails of the cabinet. At the front of the cabinet, the runners fit loosely in mortises in the stiles beside the drawers. At the back, the runner is held to the back leg with a screw. This method allows minor adjustments to be sure that the runner is square to the face of the cabinet.

After securing the runners, I used a plunge router with a fence attached to cut the grooves in the sides of the drawer boxes. Squaring the ends of the grooves with a chisel and some test fitting allowed me to fit the drawer fronts precisely. I rubbed a pencil on the edges of the runners and moved the drawers in and out several times. This marked any high spots

The drawer runners have a tenon on the front end that fits in a mortise in the stile. These are placed in position before the stile is glued in place.

The back of the drawer runner is screwed to the back leg after being squared to the front of the cabinet. A groove in the side of the drawer box lets the drawers slide nicely.

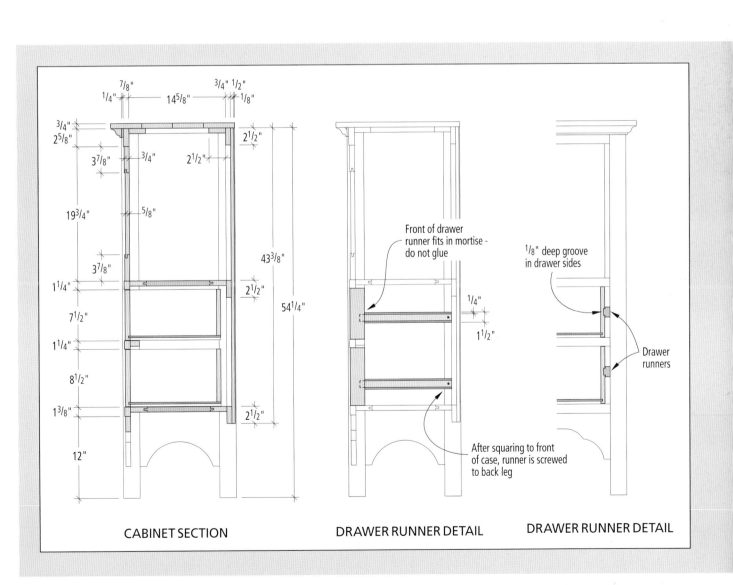

CABINET SECTION

DRAWER RUNNER DETAIL

Front of drawer runner fits in mortise - do not glue

After squaring to front of case, runner is screwed to back leg

DRAWER RUNNER DETAIL

1/8" deep groove in drawer sides

Drawer runners

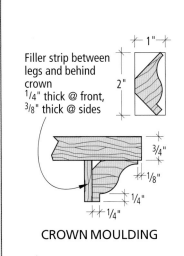

Filler strip between legs and behind crown
$\frac{1}{4}$" thick @ front,
$\frac{3}{8}$" thick @ sides

1"

2"

$\frac{3}{4}$"

$\frac{1}{8}$"

$\frac{1}{4}$"

$\frac{1}{4}$"

**CROWN MOULDING**

## Supplies

**Whitechapel Ltd.**
800-468-534 | whitechapel-ltd.com

4 ▶ 3" x 1$\frac{5}{8}$" butt hinges
#207H89P, $35.76 ea.

4 ▶ polished rosette pulls
#5PR14, $16.15 ea.

1 ▶ hollow brass knob
#98K63A, $18.97

**Lee Valley**
800-871-8158 | leevalley.com

2 ▶ ball catches
#00W12.01, $2.70 ea.

**Cornell University**
museum.cornell.edu/byrdcliffe/

▶ Byrdcliffe: An American
Arts & Crafts Colony, online exhibition

*Prices correct at time of publication.*

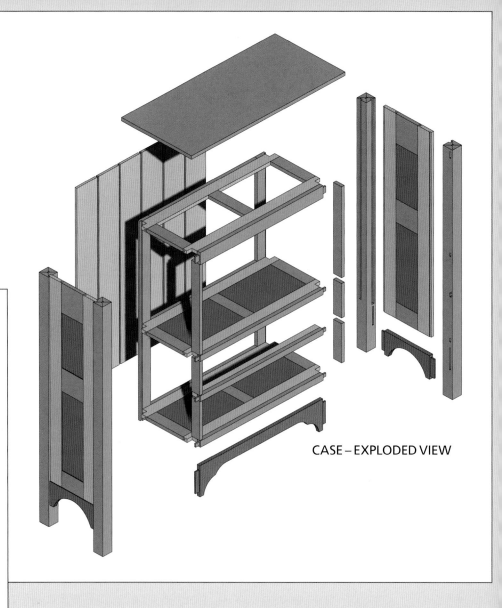

**CASE – EXPLODED VIEW**

on the runners and the grooves. I used a shoulder plane to fine-tune the fit of the drawers and runners. I then rubbed a block of paraffin on the runners to let the drawers move effortlessly.

I fit and mitered the three pieces of crown moulding together, and attached them as a unit to the cabinet. I glued the front edge in place, and attached the returns to the sides of the cabinet with a few 23-gauge pins. The top is attached to the cabinet with pan head screws through the web frame in oversized holes from below. With everything complete and fitted, I hand sanded the entire cabinet to #150 grit before staining.

## It's Not Easy Being Green

At the art supply store, I picked up two 1.25 oz. tubes of artist's oil color; one phthalo blue and one chrome yellow. To make the green stain, I mixed half of each tube together with a pallet knife on a scrap of wood and added this to a pint of natural Watco Danish Oil, an oil/varnish blend. While stirring the mixture I added one-third of a pint of mineral spirits. This turned out to be twice as much liquid as I needed, but it's better to have too much than to run out halfway through.

I applied this stain to the cabinet, saturating the surface. After letting it sit for 15 minutes, I wiped off the excess with a clean rag and allowed the stain to dry overnight. I dissasembled the doors and stained the stiles and rails separately before gluing them together so that I wouldn't get any stain on the finished panel.

The stain dries to a rich deep color and leaves some pigment in the open pores of the oak. The stain was followed with a coat of natural Watco. This coat was rubbed on sparingly with a rag. This tends to float the color off the harder, smoother areas, changing the color to more of an olive tone and highlighting the flakes and rays of the quartersawn oak. This coat was allowed to dry on the surface for 48 hours, and then the cabinet was scuffed with a Scotch-brite pad.

Some areas were a little too green, so I used some medium walnut Watco in those areas, carefully blending the color. This was allowed to dry on the surface overnight, and once dry these areas were scuffed with the abrasive pad. The entire cabinet was then given two additional coats of natural Watco, followed by a coat of paste wax.

I finished the inside of the cabinet with shellac, then installed the shiplapped back planks, screwing them at top and bottom to the cross rails of the back frame.

I wanted the hardware to look old, so I soaked it in lacquer thinner and scrubbed the finish off with a nylon abrasive pad. I then put the parts in a plastic container along with a smaller container. I poured some ammonia into the smaller container, and put the lid on the larger one. Fumes from the ammonia oxidized the hardware in a few hours, giving me the patina I wanted.

I hung the doors on the cabinet, used a pair of ball catches at the top to keep them closed, and installed the pulls and knob.

## Post Script

As a commercial enterprise, the furniture made at Byrdcliffe was a dismal failure. As examples of fine design, however, they were a tremendous success. In making this piece, I wanted to add the finest craftsmanship I could to this wonderful design, paying some respect to the anonymous craftsmen that Ralph Whitehead assumed would spoil the work if left unattended.

I knew I had succeeded when I showed my wife the finished cabinet. She looked at it for a while and then said, "It's like looking through pine trees on the edge of a forest on a perfect day in the fall." When craftsmanship evokes poetry, it's been a pretty good day.

*After staining, the wood is a rich green color and the open pores of the wood are filled with pigment.*

*The stain, a mixture of artist's oil colors and Watco Danish Oil is liberally applied. After letting it soak into the surface for 15 minutes the surface is wiped dry.*

*The stain is followed by a coat of natural color Watco, which lightens the color and highlights the figure of the quartersawn wood.*

# Greene & Greene Medicine Cabinet

## Humble origins but a distinguished pedigree combine in the ultimate Arts & Crafts medicine cabinet.

This cabinet caught my eye on my first visit to the Gamble house. I had an hour to kill before the tour began, and spent that time in the bookstore, which is housed in the original garage. Charles and Henry Greene added nice details to every facet of their work, even places the owners would rarely, if ever, see. The Gamble garage is a very nice garage.

At the back of the building is a small restroom provided for the chauffeur. That is where the original version of this cabinet has lived for almost 100 years.

I was taken with the form and proportions. The case is very simple, with curved forms on the top and bottom of the sides, and a wonderfully proportioned door. I promised myself to someday build a version.

I had a small amount of bird's-eye cherry that I had been hoarding for several years. There wasn't enough of it to build a large piece of furniture, but there was too much for a small project, so it sat in my garage. The day after completing the drawings for this project I tripped over the precious pile of cherry and decided it was time to use it. Some quick measurements revealed that I had just enough to build this cabinet.

*Vintage cabinet, special wood. Originally designed for the Gamble house a century ago by Charles and Henry Greene, this small cabinet is worthy of a prominent place in any home.*

*Quick custom jig. The dado-routing jig is made by clamping the two guide rails on either side of a shelf. The top-mounted bearing on the router bit then cuts the proper-width dado without measuring or fussing.*

*Stop action. A pencil mark indicates the end of the dado, and because the router will leave rounded ends, I stop just short of the mark.*

## Details Make Simple Into Sublime

My widest piece of cherry had enough material for the two carcase sides and the door panels. I took the piece intended for the panels, resawed it at the band saw, and set it aside while I worked on the case.

I printed full-size paper patterns of the top and bottom side profiles, and adhered them to the sides with spray adhesive. These patterns are available on page 55, or online at *popular-woodworking.com/apr09*, along with a SketchUp model of the plans.

I held the two sides together with double-stick tape, cut the profiles at the band saw, and cleaned up the cuts with a rasp followed by a scraper. Working on both sides at the same time ensured a good match, and cut the time for making the sides in half.

The top and bottom of the case fit in stopped dados. I made a jig to guide my router for cutting the dados by clamping two pieces of scrap to each side of the top. I then screwed a third piece at a right angle to the other two to register the router on the front of the case side.

Using a ⅝"-diameter mortising bit with a bearing mounted above the cutter, I made a test cut in some scrap, then clamped the jig to the side and routed a ¼"-deep dado, stopping ½" short of the width of the finished top and bottom. The top overhangs the door, and the bottom sits behind the door, so I laid out the exact dimensions before cutting the dados.

I squared off the ends of the dados with a chisel, and cut a notch in the front edge of the two horizontal pieces. The only other joinery on the case is a ½"-wide by ½"-deep rabbet for the back panels. I used a rabbeting bit in a hand-held router, cutting the rabbet along the entire length of the top and bottom. The rabbets in the sides stop where the rabbets meet the dados.

Before assembling the case, I drilled ³⁄₁₆"-diameter holes for the two adjustable shelves. I brushed the end grain of the top and bottom with yellow glue, and also coated the end grain inside the dados. After waiting 10 minutes, I brushed a second coat of glue inside the dados, and clamped the case together. Sizing the end grain like this makes for a stronger glue joint.

## A Well-made Door

The door is rather wide, and the components of it are rather thin, so I paid careful attention to the joinery. The first step was to cut a ¼"-wide by ⁵⁄₁₆"-deep groove on one edge of the outer stiles and the top and bottom rails. The narrow intermediate stiles were grooved on both edges.

I made the grooves by passing the edges of the pieces over a stack dado set at the table saw, running the grooves all the way along the edges of the stock. The groove is located ¼" in from the back of the door making it offset by ¹⁄₁₆" in the 1³⁄₁₆" material.

This meant all the grooving had to be done with the face against the saw fence, but from that point on there was no confusion regarding which was the front and which was the back on the door parts; the fat side was out and the skinny side was in.

I set up the hollow-chisel mortiser with a ¼" chisel and with the face of one of the stiles against the machine fence, I adjusted the fence so the chisel was aligned with the groove. I set the depth of the chisel to cut 1⁵⁄₁₆" deep from the edge of the stiles and cut the four mortises in the outer stiles. I wasn't sure how my material would behave, so I kept the ends of the mortises 1" away from the ends of the stiles to keep the ends from blowing out.

The top rail is the same width as the outer stiles, so the same machine settings could be used to make the mortises for the intermediate stiles. The lower rail is wider, so I had to

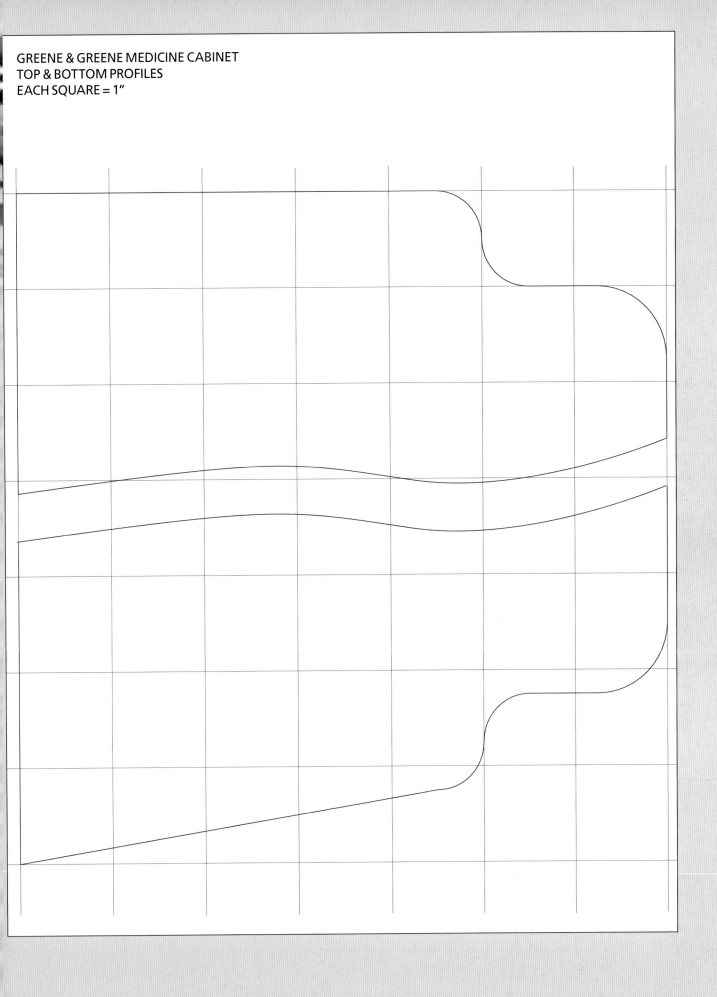

GREENE & GREENE MEDICINE CABINET
TOP & BOTTOM PROFILES
EACH SQUARE = 1"

*Finish by hand. A few cuts with a chisel complete the end of the dado for the top and bottom shelves. The front edge of the shelf is notched and ends ¹/₂" past the end of the dado. The notch is cut by hand with a dovetail saw.*

*Dual-purpose tool. The cutter on the gauge removes the remaining material where the tenon cheek and shoulder meet. After scoring it with the gauge, pare with a chisel.*

*Drop-in measurement. With the adjustable square sitting on top of the groove in the stile, the blade is bottomed out to obtain the exact measurement for the depth of the groove.*

readjust the depth of cut before cutting the last two mortises.

I used a wheel cutting gauge to define and mark the shoulders of the tenons. The fine cut left by the gauge is actually the finished edge of the shoulder. I made the cheek cuts for the tenons on the table saw using a tenoning jig that rides the saw's fence, and used the sliding crosscut table to cut the shoulders.

To avoid over-cutting the tenon shoulders, I left a little bit of material on the inside corner. I used the cutting gauge to remove this and refined the fit of the tenons with a paring

chisel and a rasp.

The groove for the panels continues beyond the tenons, so I needed to cut a haunch on the sides opposite the groove in the top and bottom rail tenons. Using my adjustable square, I set the stock on the edge of a rail, and dropped the blade into the groove.

This provided the exact dimension for the haunch without measuring. I then placed the end of the square against the shoulder and marked the cut line. After marking the width of the haunch, I made the cuts with a dovetail saw. In addition to filling in the groove, the haunch serves to keep the faces of the rails and stiles aligned.

## The Focus of Attention

The panels of the door presented an aesthetic problem. I started with one piece of material, 1³/₁₆" thick and 7" wide. I resawed it down the middle and planed the two pieces to a finished thickness of ¹/₄". My original plan was to use one piece for the center panel, and rip the other in half for the two outer panels.

The grain pattern was straight on one half of the panel, but the other half contained a cathedral arch at the bottom. The three panels together wouldn't have looked right with an arch on the left, an arch and straight grain in the center, and straight grain only on the right-hand side.

My solution was to bookmatch the panels, so I flipped one piece over, and glued the straight-grain portions together in the center. After the glue dried, I made two rip cuts in the panel, leaving a wide, straight-grained section and two narrow pieces with mirror-image arches in the lower corners.

I assembled the door in two stages. First I put the center panel in place ,and glued and clamped the two intermediate stiles between the top and bottom rails. I let this sit in the clamps over a long lunch, and then inserted the outer panels, brushed glue in the mortises of the stiles and completed the assembly.

I did this to help keep the door square. The glue on the interior joints had set, and held the top and bottom rails in position as I glued on the outer stiles. I only had to keep an eye on a few joints rather than wrestling with several clamped in opposing directions.

*Easy transfer. Setting the end of the square's blade against the shoulder, and marking with a pencil at the bottom of the stock, transfers the depth of the groove to the haunch in the tenon.*

*Faster by hand. Cutting the haunch by hand is faster than setting up to make these cuts by machine. Only the end of the haunch will be seen in the finished door, so this is a good place to practice making cuts by hand.*

## Greene & Greene Medicine Cabinet

| | NO. | ITEM | DIMENSIONS (INCHES) | | | MATERIAL | COMMENTS |
|---|---|---|---|---|---|---|---|
| | | | T | W | L | | |
| ❏ | 2 | Sides | $^{13}/_{16}$ | 7 | $27^3/_4$ | Cherry | |
| ❏ | 1 | Cabinet top | $^{13}/_{16}$ | $6^5/_8$ | 19 | Cherry | |
| ❏ | 1 | Cabinet bottom | $^{13}/_{16}$ | $5^{11}/_{16}$ | 19 | Cherry | |
| ❏ | 2 | Shelves | $^5/_8$ | $5^1/_8$ | $18^7/_{16}$ | Cherry | |
| ❏ | 4 | Back boards | $^1/_4$ | 5 | $21^3/_8$ | Cherry | Shiplapped |
| ❏ | 2 | French cleats | $^1/_4$ | 2 | $18^1/_2$ | Poplar | |
| ❏ | 2 | Outer door stiles | $^{13}/_{16}$ | 2 | $21^1/_{16}$ | Cherry | |
| ❏ | 2 | Inner door stiles | $^{13}/_{16}$ | $1^1/_4$ | $18^9/_{16}$ | Cherry | $1^1/_4$" tenon both ends |
| ❏ | 1 | Top door rail | $^{13}/_{16}$ | 2 | 17 | Cherry | $1^1/_4$" tenon both ends |
| ❏ | 1 | Bottom door rail | $^{13}/_{16}$ | 3 | 17 | Cherry | $1^1/_4$" tenon both ends |
| ❏ | 1 | Center door panel | $^1/_4$ | $6^1/_2$ | $16^9/_{16}$ | Cherry | |
| ❏ | 2 | Outer door panels | $^1/_4$ | $3^1/_2$ | $16^9/_{16}$ | Cherry | |

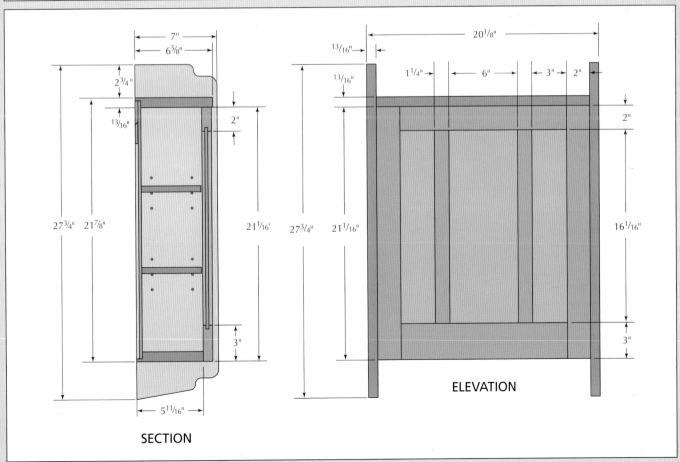

SECTION

ELEVATION

*Double duty. The haunch fills the panel groove on the outer edges of the door. It also will keep the stile and rail faces aligned if the wood warps.*

## The Search for the Right Hardware

One of the distinctive features of this cabinet is the position of the door, set back from the front of the case ½". This looks cool, but it presents a problem: There isn't any room for the barrel of standard butt hinges. The original solution was to use hinges known as "parliament hinges" commonly found on casement windows of the period.

This isn't the type of hinge likely to be found at the local hardware store, and a search of the Internet led to one source that had the correct size and configuration. The only finish

*Two step glue-up. The center panel is put in place and the intermediate stiles glued between the top and bottom rails. After letting the glue cure, the outer panels are inserted, and the stiles are glued to the rail ends.*

available was polished brass, so when the hinges arrived, I soaked them overnight in lacquer thinner, then scrubbed them with an abrasive pad.

With the finish removed, I put the hinges inside a plastic storage container with an air-tight lid. Putting on my respirator, goggles and rubber gloves, I poured a couple ounces of strong ammonia into a small cup, put that in the container along with the hinges then sealed the lid. In about two hours, the brass had the patina I was looking for.

I set a hinge on the cabinet side with the barrel even with the edge and marked a line at the bottom of the leaf. This gave a reference for the edge of the hinge mortise on the edge of the door.

I set up a small plunge router with a ½"-diameter straight bit, and set the fence so that the edge of the bit was just inside the line of the leaf edge. To set the depth of cut to the thickness of the hinge leaf, I first leveled the bottom of the bit with the base of the router. Then I placed the hinge leaf between the depth stop and the adjustment rod. Lowering the rod set the cut depth to the exact thickness.

I placed the door in my bench vise with the edge flush with a small box. This prevented the router base from tipping as I cleared the waste from the hinge mortise. A little work with a chisel cleaned out the rounded corners left by the router.

Because the barrels of the hinges are in front of the door, the door swings in a different arc than it would if hung on standard butt hinges. This allowed a narrow gap on the stile opposite the hinges, and I only needed to plane a slight back bevel to fit the door. The hinges are simply screwed to the side of the cabinet; no mortise is needed.

## Getting a Handle on Things

I had hoped to use a casement window latch to hold the door closed, as had been used on the original. A second look at the photo of the original revealed the latch actually came past the edge of the case side, with the strike plate extending about ¼" beyond the cabinet. I wasn't happy with that detail, and searched in vain for a casement latch that looked like the original without the plate sticking out.

In a moment of Krenovian inspiration, I took a scrap of cherry, 1³/₁₆" x 1" x 1¾", and sketched a profile on the side. I carefully made some rough arced cuts at the band saw, then smoothed the profiles with the round side of a rasp. I attached the handle to the door with a screw from behind, slightly below the center of the stile.

To keep the door closed, I used a small double-ball catch placed near the upper corner of the door. The bottom of the door stops on the bottom shelf. The shelves sit on 5mm-diameter pins and to keep the pins out of sight, I used a ³/₈"-diameter core box bit to rout two grooves in the bottom edge of each shelf.

*Better than measuring. Use a leaf of the hinge to set the depth stop on the plunge router. Set the bottom of the bit flush with the router base, then set the depth stop to the hinge. Plunge the router to the stop and you're set.*

*Support group. I clamp the door in my vise with the top edge of the door even with the top of a wood block. The fence on the router sets the distance for the hinge mortise, and the base of the router can't tip.*

The back consists of four ¼"-thick x 5"-wide pieces, with a rabbet on adjoining edges. These shiplapped pieces are held to the top and bottom of the cabinet with #6 x ⅝" screws. After attaching the back, I screwed a ¼"-thick French cleat across the top of the back to hold the cabinet to the wall.

My favorite finish for cherry is several coats of Danish oil, applied with a rag and wet-sanded with a nylon abrasive pad. I planed and scraped all of the cabinet parts before assembly, to keep sanding to a minimum. Before finishing, I hand-sanded with #240-grit Abranet, then sanded again with #320-grit, leaving a smooth surface.

I wanted to warm and darken the color so I used Watco "Medium Walnut" for the first three coats of finish. I flooded the surface for the first coat, and kept the surface wet for 45 minutes, adding oil to any areas that dried out. Then with a clean rag, I wiped the surface dry, and left things alone for a couple hours.

The second coat can be applied the same day as the first, but I only left it wet for 15 or 20 minutes before wiping it dry. This and subsequent coats were left to dry overnight. Three coats of "Natural" Watco followed the first three coats, and after 48 hours of drying, I applied a coat of paste wax. The completed cabinet is destined for a nicer home than the back of the garage.

## Supplies

**Hardware Source**
877-944-6437 | hardwaresource.com

2 ▶ brass parliament hinges, 2¼" x 3"
  #817000, $15.97 each

**Lee Valley**
800-871-8158 | leevalley.com

1 ▶ double ball catch, 38mm x 7mm
  #00W12.00, $1.80

8 ▶ steel shelf supports,
  #00S10.01, $4.20 pkg. of 50

*Prices correct at time of publication.*

*Final cuts. The router leaves a flat bottom and a straight back edge to the hinge mortise. The rounded corners, however, need to be removed with a chisel. Knifed-in layout lines provide a reference for the chisel.*

# Craftsman Bookcase

## If something is worth doing, it's worth doing excessively.

There are many bookcases in my house, but they're a motley collection – poor cousins to the rest of the furniture. The really nice bookcases I've made have gone to live with clients, while I have kept the prototypes and the also-rans. They are nicer than concrete blocks and pine planks, but not my best work. The cherry bookcase in my living room was a test case – both of a dovetail jig and the wood's moisture content.

It was time for something nicer. This design is an adaptation of early 20th-century Gustav Stickley bookcases. I wanted to use nice wood, and show off a bit with the joinery.

I didn't have a specific species of wood in mind when I went to the lumberyard, but I knew I wanted something attractive and wide enough to avoid gluing up individual boards. I found a nice batch of sapele, also known as African mahogany, and brought home 50 board feet of wide planks.

*Dedicated jig. This dado jig is made to fit the thickness of the shelves, and utilizes a flush-cutting bit with the bearin g on top.*

## Off to a Good Start

My lumber had been surfaced to $1\frac{5}{16}$", but it wasn't quite flat. After cutting the parts to rough sizes, I ran the material over the jointer and through the planer to remedy that, ending up with stock slightly thicker than $1\frac{3}{16}$". I planed off the mill marks with a smoothing plane, and dressed all of the stock with a scraper before working on the joinery.

This exercise served two purposes: I now knew the material was straight and true, and having the faces at a nearly finished state would save work later on. It's a lot easier to work on a plank on a bench than it is to work inside an assembled cabinet.

When the faces were smooth, I cut the sides and fixed shelves to their final sizes. I determined which side should be right and which should be left, situating the most attractive faces on the outside. I put a 1"-diameter straight bit in my plunge router, and set the fence to cut a $\frac{7}{8}$"-wide, $\frac{1}{2}$"-deep rabbet on the back edge of each side, stopping at the bottom edge of the lowest shelf.

Doing this step first established the sides as right and left, and it kept me from confusing the inside and outside faces as I worked on the remaining joints. Each of the three shelves connects to the cabinet sides with a pair of wedged through-tenons. On the inside of the case, each shelf sits in a $\frac{1}{8}$"-deep dado.

The dados aren't really needed structurally, but they ensure that the inner surfaces of the joints always look good, and they help to locate the through-mortises with the jigs that I used. With a dozen through-mortises to fit, I needed a method to make the process efficient and idiot-resistant, if not idiot-proof.

## Jigs and Joints Work Together

Because I didn't have a router bit the exact size to match the thickness of the shelves, I decided to use a $\frac{5}{8}$"-diameter, $\frac{1}{2}$

$\frac{1}{2}$"-long bit with a guide bearing mounted above the cutters. I made a jig to match the thickness of the shelves by clamping an offcut from one of the shelves between the two fences.

I then screwed a straight piece of scrap to one end of the fences, making certain that the inner edge was square to the working edges of the fences. I screwed another piece of scrap to the opposite end of the fences, and I was ready to make a test cut. The resulting dado was just a bit narrow, and a few swipes with the smoothing plane on the bottom of the shelves made for a snug fit.

After routing the three dados in each of the case sides, I began to make the second jig, which is used to cut the mortises. The mortises are $\frac{5}{8}$" wide and $2\frac{3}{4}$" long, and they are equal distances from the front and back of the case sides with a 3" space in between. Rather than cut the mortises in the jig, I made them by assembling pieces of $\frac{1}{2}$"-thick plywood in two layers.

I laid out the locations of the mortises on the larger, bottom part of the jig, then I glued and nailed smaller pieces along the layout lines. I drilled holes in the waste area, and with a flush-trim bit in my router, I trimmed the bottom of the jig to match the top. A few cuts with a chisel to clean out the corners and I was ready to make mortises – almost.

The mortises need to be exactly centered in the dados, and I needed a way for the jig to be clamped to the case sides. I made an edge piece the thickness of the case side, plus the thickness of the jig, and used the same jig that I used to cut the dados in the sides to cut a notch across this piece. This notch aligns the jig to the shelf dados.

After carefully centering this piece on the mortises, I screwed it in place and made a test cut. I used an offcut from one of the shelves to align the jig for routing. I jammed the offcut in the dado in the case side, leaving an inch or so protruding from the edge of the side. This allowed me to knock the notch in the jig over the scrap. With the jig properly aligned to the case side, I clamped it in place. After drilling a hole to get the bit started, I cut the mortises with a flush-trim bit in my router.

After routing each pair of mortises, I left the jig clamped in place, flipped the side over and used the jig as a guide to cut the corners of the mortises square with a chisel.

At this point, I walked away from mortise-and-tenon territory and went to work on the curved profiles at the top front corner of each side, and the arched cutouts at the bottom. After laying out the curves on one side, I cut close to the line with a jigsaw and cleaned up the edges with a rasp.

The first side was put into service as a template for the second. I put the finished side on top of the other and traced the curves. After cutting the curves in the second side, I clamped the two together, and used a flush-cutting bit in the router to make the second side an exact match of the first.

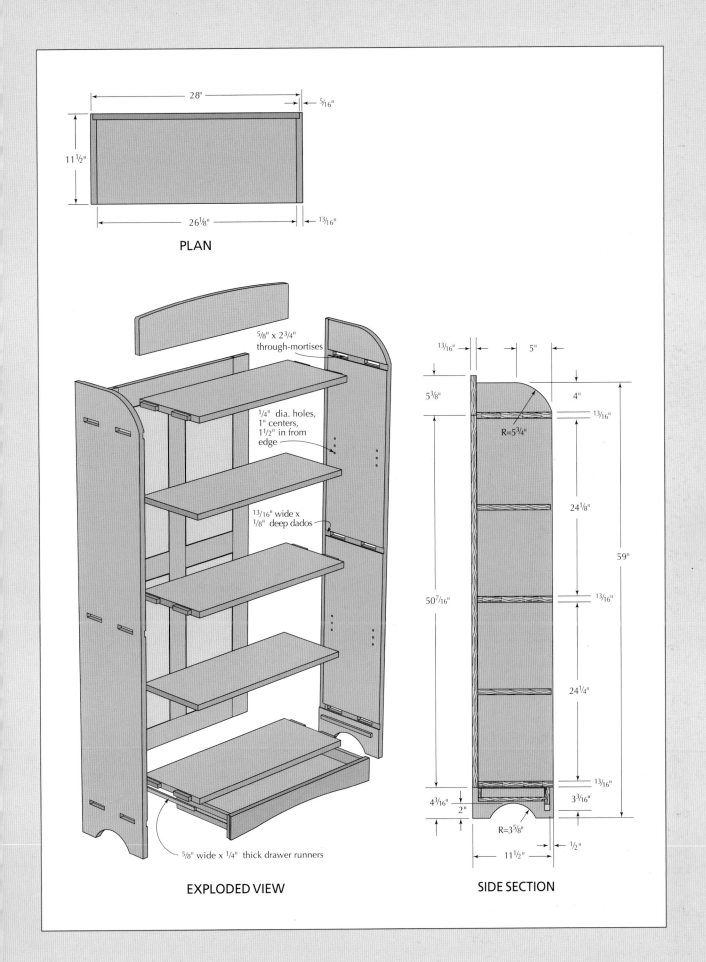

28"

5/16"

11 1/2"

26 1/8"

13/16"

PLAN

5/8" x 2 3/4"
through-mortises

1/4" dia. holes,
1" centers,
1 1/2" in from
edge

13/16" wide x
1/8" deep dados

5/8" wide x 1/4" thick drawer runners

EXPLODED VIEW

13/16"

5"

5 3/8"

4"

R=5 3/4"

13/16"

24 1/8"

59"

50 7/16"

13/16"

24 1/4"

13/16"

4 3/16"

3 3/16"

2"

R=3 5/8"

1/2"

11 1/2"

SIDE SECTION

## A Trip to Through-Tenon Territory

The next step is where the dados in the case sides saved a tremendous amount of time and prevented the formation of even more grey hair. The layout for the tenons needs to match the mortise locations exactly.

At this point I looked at the three shelves, marked the best face and edge of each, and decided which one would be the top, middle and bottom. I clamped the entire cabinet together and with a lumber crayon, marked the locations of the shelves in relation to the cabinet sides.

Some hand fitting would be needed, and putting a carefully fit bottom shelf upside down in the top shelf location wouldn't be a good thing. With the case together, I ran the point of my knife around the perimeter of each mortise, marking the location of the tenons in the ends of the shelves.

I set up a small plunge router with a fence set to leave the tenons slightly proud of the outside of the cabinet sides. I set the depth to the top of the knife marks, checking both sides of each end to be sure that the tenons were centered. I wanted to make the cheek cuts quickly, but I didn't want to go too far.

I cut the edge cheeks of the tenons with a dovetail saw, and used a jigsaw to remove the waste between the two

## Craftsman Bookcase

| | NO. | ITEM | DIMENSIONS (INCHES) | | | MATERIAL | COMMENTS |
|---|---|---|---|---|---|---|---|
| | | | T | W | L | | |
| ❏ | 2 | Sides | $^{13}/_{16}$ | $11^1/_2$ | 59 | Sapele | |
| ❏ | 3 | Fixed shelves | $^{13}/_{16}$ | $10^{11}/_{16}$ | $28^1/_8$ | Sapele | |
| ❏ | 2 | Adjustable shelves | $^{13}/_{16}$ | $10^7/_{16}$ | $26^1/_4$ | Sapele | |
| ❏ | 2 | Back panel outer stiles | $^{13}/_{16}$ | $3^5/_{16}$ | $50^7/_{16}$ | Sapele | |
| ❏ | 1 | Back panel inner stile | $^{13}/_{16}$ | 3 | $46^5/_{16}$ | Sapele | $1^1/_4$" TBE * |
| ❏ | 1 | Back panel top rail | $^{13}/_{16}$ | 3 | $23^1/_4$ | Sapele | $1^1/_4$" TBE * |
| ❏ | 1 | Back panel bottom rail | $^{13}/_{16}$ | $3^5/_8$ | $23^1/_4$ | Sapele | $1^1/_4$" TBE * |
| ❏ | 2 | Back panel middle rails | $^{13}/_{16}$ | 3 | $11^3/_8$ | Sapele | $1^1/_4$" TBE * |
| ❏ | 4 | Back panels | $^3/_4$ | $9^5/_8$ | $21^1/_8$ | Sapele | |
| ❏ | 1 | Back splash | $^{13}/_{16}$ | $5^3/_8$ | $27^1/_2$ | Sapele | |
| ❏ | 1 | Lower apron/drawer front | $^{13}/_{16}$ | $3^3/_{16}$ | $26^3/_8$ | Sapele | |
| ❏ | 2 | Drawer sides | $^5/_8$ | $1^3/_4$ | $10^1/_{16}$ | Maple | |
| ❏ | 1 | Drawer back | $^1/_2$ | $1^1/_4$ | $26^1/_8$ | Maple | |
| ❏ | 1 | Drawer bottom | $^1/_2$ | $9^3/_4$ | $25^3/_8$ | Poplar | |
| ❏ | 2 | Drawer runners | $^3/_8$ | $^3/_4$ | $9^1/_{16}$ | Maple | |

*\* TBE=Tenon both ends*

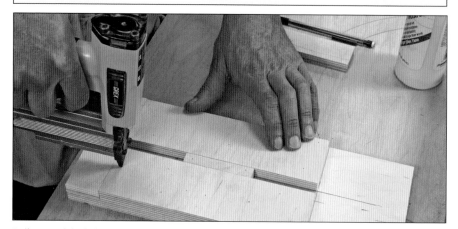

*Built around the holes. This jig for the through-mortises is made by assembling small pieces to a backer. The openings are then cut with a router and a locating fence is added.*

*Double duty. After routing, the mortising jig also serves as a guide for the chisel to square the corners of the through-mortises.*

tenons. With the end of each shelf housed in the dado these cuts didn't need to be pretty; I only needed to get material out of the way.

Before starting the fitting process, I took a chisel and chamfered the inside edge of each mortise, and with a piece of sandpaper I broke the sharp edge of each tenon to prevent damge to the outside of the mortises during fitting.

With a soft pencil, I made a series of hatch marks on the tenon cheeks and eased them into place. When I met resistance, I removed the shelf and examined the marks. The tight spots showed as smears in the pencil lines and I used a float to reduce the thickness until I had a good fit.

## A Further Complication

Clearly in the grips of an obsessive-compulsive exposed-joinery episode, I laid out each tenon end for a pair of wedges. Un-

Getting in shape. After cutting the lower arch with a jigsaw, the curve is smoothed with a rasp.

One side makes another. After the curves on one side are completed, the first side is used as a template to make the second side.

able to leave well enough alone, I decided it would look nice to set the wedges on a slight angle, making dovetail-like shapes in the end of each tenon.

I marked the distance to the edge of each cut on the ends of the tenons with a combination square, then marked the angles with a bevel gauge and knife. The slots for the wedges are at a compound angle, but I only fussed about the start of each cut. Using a dovetail saw, I cut the vertical angles by eye.

This meant that the wedges also had to be a complex shape. I began by cutting simple wedges from a piece of purpleheart, about 1" thick, 8" wide and 1½" long. I set the miter gauge on the band saw to 3° and made the wedges by making a cut, flipping the wood over and making a second cut.

I put each wedge in place, trimmed off the end with a saw, then pared the edges with a chisel to match the tenon cheeks. To keep the wedges organized, after fitting a group I stuck them in order on a strip of blue painter's tape, then stuck the tape to the face of each shelf. On final assembly, each group of wedges would be where they belonged.

For assembly, I used liquid hide glue to allow plenty of open

time to put the joints together and set the wedges in place. After clamping the assembly, I brushed glue in each slot then drove the wedges in with a hammer. While the glue was drying, I made the back panel.

This panel is straightforward: The rails and stiles join with mortises and tenons that are haunched at the top and bottom extremes to fill the grooves for the panels. The panels are slightly thinner than the frame, and they are raised on both sides. The panel was made about 1/16" too wide to allow for fitting to the case, and the top is trimmed to land in the center of the top shelf.

## Back to Level Ground

When the glue on the case had completely dried, it was time to trim the wedges and exposed tenons down to the surface of the case sides. The first step was to use a flush-cutting saw to remove the ends of the wedges. Then I took a rag soaked with mineral spirits, and wet the ends of the tenons.

This saturation makes the tough end-grain fibers easier to trim with a block plane. The final bit of leveling was with a

Marked in place. The tenons are marked directly from the mortises, ensuring that the locations match.

Shoulders first. A shallow rabbet is cut on each side of the shelves to start the making of the tenons.

Ends second. The ends of the tenons are cut by hand, then the waste in between is removed.

*Test, don't guess. Penciled hatch marks on the tenons will smear and reveal tight spots within the joints during the test fitting.*

*A little off the top. The pencil lines smear where material needs to be removed. A planemaker's float gives good control and leaves a smooth surface.*

*How it ought to be. The ends can be a bit loose because the wedges will expand the tenons.*

card scraper and when the tenons were flush, I scraped the entire surface of both cabinet sides.

I had set aside a small piece of stock for the backsplash. The grain on this piece arched to match the profile I intended to cut, and with the back in place in the carcase, I trimmed it to final width and length, then marked the curved top edge. After cutting the shape on the band saw, I removed the saw marks with my block plane and shaped the corners with a rasp where the splash meets the case sides.

## I've Got a Secret

The arched apron below the lowest shelf also was selected with the curve of the grain centered on the cut-out shape. The apron attaches to the cabinet in an unusual way. It actually is the front of a hidden drawer.

The apron is 1/16" shorter than the distance between the two sides of the cabinet, and the 5/8"-thick maple drawer sides are 1 3/4" wide and 10 1/4" long. The sides join the drawer front with half-blind dovetails, and are set in from the ends about 1/8" on each side. A 1/4"-wide, 1/8"-deep groove was cut in the outer face of each drawer side after the drawer was assembled to hang the drawer on runners.

The drawer runners are strips of maple, 3/4" wide x 1/4" thick, held to the cabinet sides with screws. The reason for setting the drawer sides in was to leave the smallest possible gap between the ends of the drawer front and the cabinet

*One size fits all. In theory, the tapered wedges will fit anywhere. In reality, I fit each one and kept them in order.*

sides, and to make the runners a substantial thickness.

A small rabbeted lip is left on the end grain of the drawer front, so that any trimming needed to fit the front would be on this small edge. I'd seen a similar detail on an original drawer, and was curious to see if it would be as easy to trim and fit as it first appeared. The final fitting was indeed easier, but this complicated the drawer construction.

I cut the dovetail joints at the front and made the sockets between the pins 1/8" deeper than the thickness of the drawer sides. After fitting the pieces, I took them apart, and cut the rabbets on the ends of the drawer front at the table saw. When I was satisfied with the joints at the front of the drawer, I cut the drawer back to length, then cut the through-dovetails at the rear of the drawer's sides.

Setting the sides of the drawer in from the ends of the drawer front posed a problem for letting in the groove for the drawer runners. I used a small router with a fence to cut the grooves, but had to temporarily attach thin pieces of scrap on each side of the groove location to keep the base of the router above the end of the drawer front's lip.

After cutting the grooves, I carefully measured back 1" from the inside edge of the rabbet on each side. The fence on the router left the grooves short of this, so I used a chisel to extend the groove to this line, squaring up the end of the groove in the process. It's important that the grooves end at the same point, so that the ends of the runners can act as drawer stops.

I cut the maple runners and fit them to the width of the grooves in the drawer sides. Gravity will keep the top edge of the groove in contact with the runner, so the runner can be

sized to slide easily. I left a margin of 1/32" so that the drawer won't bind if the runner swells in width.

After fitting the width, I planed the faces of the runners until the combined width of the drawer and runners with both runners in place was 1/16" less than the inside of the cabinet. There needs to be some room to allow for easy movement of the drawer, but not so much as to make the drawer sloppy.

The drawer bottom is 1/2" thick, and slides into 1/4"-wide, 1/4"-deep grooves in the insides of the drawer sides and front. I used the same setup on the router table for raising the back panels to form the tongue on three edges of the drawer bottom. The back of the drawer is 1/2" narrower than the sides to allow the bottom to slide in after the drawer is assembled. A couple screws in elongated holes secure the thick back edge of the bottom to the drawer back and allow for seasonal wood movement.

With the drawer completely assembled, I measured in from the front of the case 2 5/16" (the 1 3/16" thickness of the drawer front, plus the 1" distance from the back of the front to the end of the groove in the side, plus the 1/4" set-back of the drawer front from the front of the case).

I measured down from the bottom of the lowest shelf and

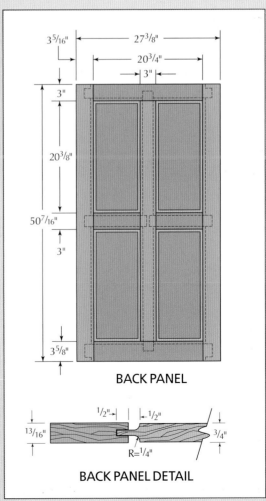

**BACK PANEL**

**BACK PANEL DETAIL**

*The easy part. Each wedge is pared flush with the surrounding tenon. Then they are removed and stuck to a piece of blue painter's tape.*

*Soak then shave. After sawing off the wedges, the joints are soaked with paint thinner to make it easier to trim the end grain flush.*

*At the same level. Following the plane, a scraper is used to smooth the exposed tenon ends and the cabinet sides.*

*Sliding home. The drawer bottom slides past the drawer back and into grooves in the sides and front. Screws in elongated holes will hold the bottom to the back and allow the bottom to shrink or swell.*

*No one will ever know. Located below the shelf and 1/2" back from the front edge, the drawer appears to be a fixed apron.*

*Now you see it. The rabbet in the end of the drawer front provides clearance for the sides, while allowing a narrow margin to be trimmed easily.*

drew a line parallel to the shelf to locate the runner. With the drawer front 1/2" behind the edge of the shelf, the top of the drawer front can't be seen when it is closed, so I left a 1/16" gap so the drawer wouldn't scrape the shelf on its way in and out. When I had the positions of the runners located, I screwed them to the inside of the case with #6 x 5/8" flathead screws.

## Easy Elbow Grease Finish

Because I had planed and scraped all the large flat surfaces before assembly, there wasn't much to be done to get ready for finishing the bookcase. I planed the front edges of the fixed shelves flush to the cabinet sides, chamfered all of the edges slightly with a block plane, and gave everything a light sanding with #240 grit.

The first coat of finish was Watco Light Walnut Danish Oil. I saturated the surface, wet-sanded it with a nylon abrasive pad, kept the surface wet for about 45 minutes, then wiped off the excess. This was followed by two coats a day of Waterlox for three days. After allowing the finish to cure for a couple days, I wet-sanded it with Watco Satin Wax and #400 grit wet/dry paper, leaving a nice sheen and a surface that is pleasant to the touch.

The joinery, details and finish on this bookcase are more than what is needed to store some books, but that really wasn't the purpose in making it. The idea was to leave something behind that demonstrates what a bit of extra effort looks like. It makes me look like a competent craftsman. Now to fill it with some books that might make me look intelligent, as well.

*Hidden away. The hidden drawer rides on wooden slides attached to the carcase. The end of the groove will act as a stop for the runners, and needs to end in the right spot.*

*Simple enough. Maple runners below the bottom shelf support and guide the hidden drawer.*

# Stickley Book Rack

## Expose your joinery skills with this Arts & Crafts classic.

In the early 1900s, furniture maker Gustav Stickley began producing a unique style of furniture that he called "Craftsman." At the time, the world was coming into the modern industrial age, and Stickley, among others, began to question the value of mass-produced furniture and its effect on those who made or owned it.

Victorian furniture featured many machine-made elements that sought to mimic the handwork of earlier times. In most cases these adornments detracted rather than added. Just because machines could produce intricate imitation carvings and mouldings didn't mean that they should. Stickley decided to get back to basics.

This simple book rack is a good example of the style. The joinery, along with the character of the quartersawn white oak, becomes the decoration. Function comes first, and the form is a combination of nice wood, good proportions and honest joinery.

Making this piece is like going to Craftsman boot camp. You'll get to know the nature of the wood and how to make exposed joints. It's not a big piece, but there are enough joints and details to provide plenty of practice.

Craftsman furniture was factory made, but Stickley's aim was to use machines to save the workers from drudgery while providing room to display skilled workmanship. At the time, most of the machines we know today were in common use, but the subtle details that make this piece special have to be completed by hand.

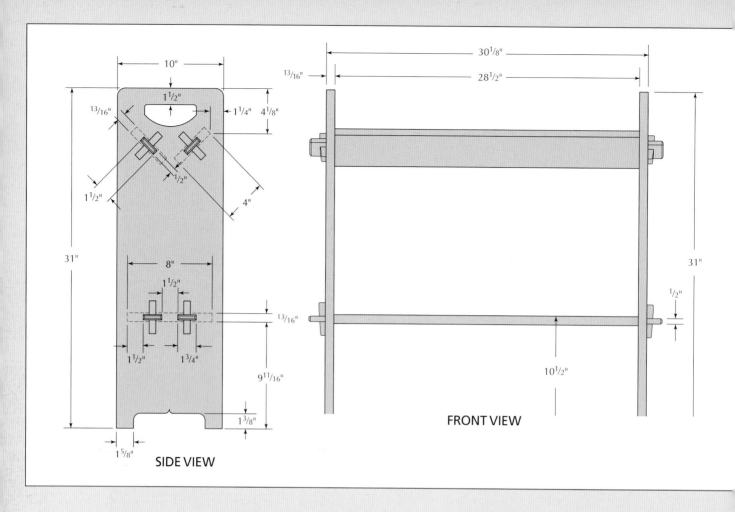

**SIDE VIEW**

**FRONT VIEW**

We have the choice to work by hand, work by power or work with both. If we understand where each method excels – as well as where each falls short – we can master both sides and produce furniture we're proud of, without taking forever to make it.

## Precision & Productivity

The heart of this piece is the keyed through-mortise-and-tenon joinery. There are eight of these joints to make, each with two through-mortises. One of the givens in this type of work is consistency, and the electric router, combined with the precision of a template, provides that.

I print a full-size pattern of the side profiles and joint locations, and attach the prints to a piece of ½"-thick Baltic birch plywood with spray adhesive. These patterns are available online in PDF format at *http://www.popularwoodworking.com/ projects/furniture-plans/arts-and-crafts-furniture/stickley-book- rack-stickley-plans.*

I use a straightedge and an X-Acto knife to mark the lines of the mortises from the pattern. Then I remove the pattern, drill a 7/16"-diameter hole at each mortise location and place

double-sided tape over the lines. That allows me to place small pieces of plywood along the lines. The adhesive is pressure-sensitive, so I smack the pieces with a mallet to fix them in position.

With the pattern pieces in place, I use a ⅜" bearing-guided flush-trim bit to cut the openings exactly on the layout lines. After routing, I peel off the pattern pieces and remove the residue left by the tape with lacquer thinner.

The router makes straight and parallel edges, but leaves round corners that must be squared with a chisel. To make the D-shaped handle opening at the top of the pattern I drill a hole at both ends of the top edge, and cut the curve with a jigsaw. The edges of this opening are then cleaned up with a rasp.

Why bother cleaning up the corners of the template when the router will also leave round corners on the workpiece? The router does a good job of making straight edges, but can tear out the solid wood. I score the grain on the work with a knife and a chisel to prevent that.

I cut the sides to finished size and then make a rough cut with the jigsaw at the top opening to lessen the load on the router and bit. Then I clamp the template to the side, and clamp both to an open-ended box on my bench. This holds

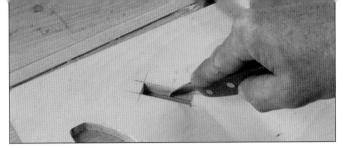

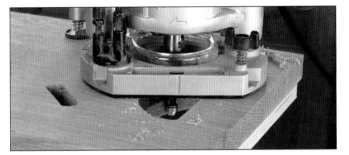

*Score first. Prevent tear-out by scoring around the openings before cutting with the router.*

*Saw first, then trim. Cut close to the lines with a jigsaw and use the router to trim the opening at the top.*

*Swing it. Press the back of the chisel against the mortise wall, then rotate the edge down to the corner to maintain a straight edge.*

*On top. Positioning your shoulder over the chisel allows you to use your body weight to pare the end of the mortise.*

the work at a comfortable height and I run the router around the inside perimeter of each opening.

## Chisel Time

After the noise and flying chips of routing, cleaning up the corners with a chisel and float is a nice change of pace. I hone a fresh edge on a wide chisel, and place the flat back face on the long routed edge. Then I rotate the chisel down and into the corner to begin the squaring process. This keeps the chisel from drifting past the layout lines as I make the cuts.

I alternate cuts with a chisel that matches the width of the mortise and the wide chisel until the corners are complete. All of this takes place with the outside face of the side facing up. Any tear-out or chips will be hidden by the shoulder of the tenoned shelf. A flat float is used to put the finishing touches on the mortises.

## All in a Row

After cutting the three shelves to finished size, I place them beside each other on the bench and mark all of the shoulders

at once using a large square. This ensures that the distance between the shoulders is consistent. Then I take a smaller square with a metal rule and knife in the shoulder lines all around each piece.

In theory, the mortises are all exactly ½" wide, but in reality there will be some variation. I place the end of one of the narrow shelves next to a mortise to gauge the width directly from one part to the other. I set the shelf end on one long edge and mark where the other edge of the mortise hits.

I set my marking gauge by eye to the middle of the distance from the pencil mark to the edge of the shelf. I then mark with the gauge from opposite faces of the shelf, and make any needed adjustments until the tenon layout matches the mortise. When I have the setting right, I mark around the ends of the tenons with the gauge.

This seems like extra work, but the cut layout lines won't rub off, and they help to prevent tear-out as the tenons are cut and fitted. The layout marks will be the visible edges when the joint is finished. Tenons look simple, but there are several cuts to be made.

I cut the shoulders with a backsaw. The shoulders are only

# Stickley No. 74 Book Rack

| | NO. | ITEM | DIMENSIONS (INCHES) | | | MATERIAL | COMMENTS |
|---|---|---|---|---|---|---|---|
| | | | T | W | L | | |
| ❑ | 2 | Ends | $^{13}/_{16}$ | 10 | 31 | QSWO* | |
| ❑ | 1 | Lower shelf | $^{13}/_{16}$ | 8 | 33$^5/_8$ | QSWO | 1$^3/_4$" TBE* |
| ❑ | 2 | Upper shelves | $^{13}/_{16}$ | 4 | 33$^5/_8$ | QSWO | 1$^3/_4$" TBE |
| ❑ | 8 | Keys | $^5/_8$ | $^5/_8$ | 5 | QSWO | Trim after fitting |

*QSWO=Quartersawn White Oak, TBE=Tenon Both Ends*

about ⅛" deep, and a fine-toothed saw leaves a nice, clean edge. There are a several ways to make the cheek cuts, and on the narrow shelves the cheeks could be cut on the band saw.

The cheeks on the lower shelf are too wide for a small band saw, so I remove the material with a straight bit on the router table. This leaves a consistent flat surface across the wide board. These tenons need to fit neatly, but one of the challenges is that the last cut is the visible surface in the finished piece. I rout close, but fine-tune the fit by hand.

*On your mark. Use the mortise to determine the exact thickness of the tenon.*

*Get set. Set the gauge to half the distance between the pencil line and the edge.*

## A Different Rout

I begin the setup by raising the top of the bit to the bottom of the layout lines on the ends of the shelves. There is some trial and error here, so it is best to begin with a fat tenon, then make minor adjustments until the machined corner of the tenon will just fit in a mortise. Adjustments to the cut are tiny, because the cuts are made on both sides of the piece. The difference is twice the amount of the height adjustment.

I set my combination square to the distance from the end of the tenon to the shoulder, then use the square to set the router table fence. I've already made the finished shoulder cut, so I set the router bit to just meet the saw kerf. The first pass is made with the end of the board against the fence. I use a wide backing board to push the material across the bit and move the board out with each pass.

When the cheeks are the proper thickness, I place the end of each shelf on end next to its mortise. I mark all the joints with a lumber crayon so that I keep the arrangement of the parts the same as I fit each joint. I mark the end cuts with a pencil, then use the combination square to carry those lines back to the shoulder.

I make the tenon end cuts for the narrow shelves with a band saw, and stop just before the blade reaches the edge of the shoulder.

On the wide shelf, material between the two tenons must be removed. I make a rough cut at the band saw, and aim wide on these cuts so that when I remove the band-saw marks I don't end up beyond the layout lines. I set a guide bearing on a flush-trim bit in the router to ride on the pre-cut edge of the shoulder and use the router to clean up the junk between

*Check & go. Mark from both sides to center the tenon and adjust until the parts match.*

*Rise to the challenge. Set the cutter to the bottom of the layout line.*

*Got your back. Use a wide block to move the narrow shelves across the router bit.*

the tenons back to the shoulder line.

## Fit to be Fit

In a perfect world, the tenons would slide neatly into the mortises at this point, and I would move on to the next step. In real life, however, it isn't that easy. There needs to be a slight amount of clearance to assemble the joint, but not so much as to leave a visible gap on the outside. The prudent course is to make the tenon just a bit big, then reduce its size in controlled, small amounts.

Before fitting the joints, I take a chisel and bevel both the ends of the tenons, and the inside edges of the mortises. This makes it easier to slide the tenons in, and it prevents the hard edges of the tenons from breaking the edges of the mortises as they exit.

I start with the narrow top shelves with the single tenons, and I push the piece in as far as I can. I remove the tenon and look for dents or shiny spots that indicate where material needs to be removed. It's easier to remove material from the tenon, and depending on how much needs to be removed I will use a chisel, shoulder plane or a float.

Before the second attempt at fitting, I take a soft pencil and make hatch marks on the tenon. Then I shove the pieces back together. The pencil marks smear on the high spots, and I'll work on those with the float. The mortises shouldn't need any work, but sometimes there will be a bump on the inside walls that has to be removed, so I always take a good look at both parts of the joint.

It's tempting to break out the mallet and start pounding away, but it is safer to work on the joints with hand pressure only. Banging can split the side piece, especially if it has been glued up from

*Now you know. Aim for a snug fit by testing a corner of the tenon in the mortise after routing the cheeks.*

*From the source. Mark the ends of the tenons directly from the mortises.*

*Stop in time. Cut the end of the tenon, but stop just short of your shoulder line.*

Off the top. The pencil marks indicate the high spots. Remove them with a float, then test the fit again.

Ease in. Bevel both the ends of the tenons and the edges of the mortises for fitting.

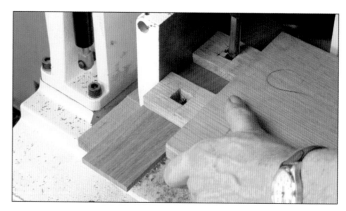

Back it up. A thin piece of scrap under the tenon provides support when making the second mortise.

## Shop Drawings for Craftsman Furniture

In 2001, my first book, "Shop Drawings for Craftsman Furniture," was published by Cambium Press (now Fox Chapel). I had been a fan of Gustav Stickley designs since the start of my woodworking career, and I was tired of seeing misguided interpretations and watered-down imitations of this wonderful furniture presented as authentic.

My idea was to show detailed drawings of original pieces, along with text pertinent to making good reproductions, and a brief history of those who made the originals. That book was a success, and it was followed by "More Shop Drawings for Craftsman Furniture" and "Shop Drawings for Craftsman Inlays and Hardware" (both from Fox Chapel).

Those three books are now combined in a new, single edition titled "Great Book of Shop Drawings for Craftsman Furniture" (Fox Chapel). The new book contains all of the drawings for 57 different pieces of furniture from the original books, drawings for authentic hardware and the inlay designs produced for Gustav Stickley by Harvey Ellis. The introductory text has been combined and updated and there are many new photos of both vintage pieces and the steps for making reproductions.

If you're among the many woodworkers who enjoy this style of American furniture, this is a comprehensive resource for understanding these designs, and building pieces of your own.

narrower pieces and is weak near the opening at the top.

The lower shelf is worked the same way, but it is trickier to fit both tenons at the same time. Each round of fitting and trimming requires some detective work to find out exactly what is keeping the joint from going home. When all the tenons have been fit, the shelves should fit snug and square.

## Mortises, Take Two

I lay out the secondary mortises by marking the outside of the upright on the tenon. Then I set my combination square to leave a ⅝" opening when marked from each side. Then I make a mark ⁹⁄₁₆" away from the upright, parallel to the first mark.

The mortise is initially cut at ⅝" square, with the inner edge set ¹⁄₁₆" behind the outer face of the upright. This ensures that the wedge holds the joint tight, no matter what kind of swelling or shrinking may take place over time. The mortise can be cut with one pass of a ⅝" hollow-mortise chisel, or four passes with a ⅜" chisel.

Cut a piece of scrap to match the height of the shoulder so that the tenon isn't hanging in space at the mortise machine. Set the fence of the machine to the exposed outer end of the mortise and make the cuts. Reset the fence to cut the back edges. The outer edge of the mortise is angled by hand to match the angle of the wedge.

I don't worry about the angle; I make a sloping cut that starts 1/16" away from the layout line. I mark the line, then press my chisel against the wall of the mortise and swing the edge down to the corner. Then I stand facing the tenon, put the edge of the chisel on the line and angle it back by sighting down the back of the chisel to the edge of the mortise below.

After tidying up the edges of the small mortises, I cut 5/8"-square pieces a few inches longer than needed for the

*Angle by eye. Use a chisel to taper the end of the mortise for the wedge.*

*Just behind. The square end of the mortise lies behind the face of the side to allow the wedge to seat tightly.*

wedges. I carry the layout lines from the mortise to an edge of the tenons, and mark the slope on each wedge from the marks on the tenon. I make the angled cuts on the band saw, then remove the saw marks with a few swipes of a block plane.

The wedges are seated by tapping them gently with a mallet. The sound changes when they are tight. If you hit the wedges too hard, it's easy to break out the end of the tenon. Should that happen, the broken piece can be glued back in place.

When the wedges fit nicely, I mark an equal distance above and below the tenon, and cut them to length. I make a discrete mark on both the wedge and the inside of the mortise so the wedges will go back in the same holes to which they were fit.

## After Everything Fits

After completing the joinery, the book rack is taken apart for finishing. All the parts are exposed, and need to have the edges eased and surfaces smoothed. The curved portions of the cutout at the top and the scroll at the bottom of the sides are smoothed with rasps.

I put a slight bevel on the edges of the shelves and sides using a block plane for the long edges and a fine rasp for the curved parts. I remove any mill marks from the faces of the boards with a smooth plane. The ends of the tenons and the wedges are also eased, starting where these pieces exit their mortises. The chamfers on these edges gradually increase the farther away they get from adjacent surfaces.

Original pieces were ammonia-fumed, then shellacked. I used a combination of oil stain, walnut Danish Oil and shellac for a similar look.

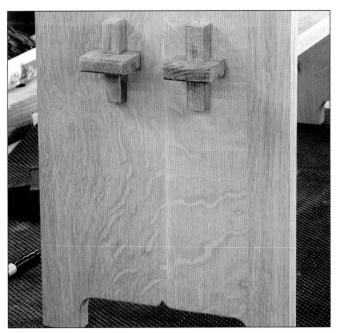

*Hard & soft. Edges on the tenons and keys are beveled, but they fade away to leave clean lines at the joints.*

# Authentic Stickley Finish

For the August 2012 issue of *Popular Woodworking Magazine*, I built a reproduction of a Gustav Stickley No. 74 Book Rack. It's a great piece in a couple of ways: It is useful and nice looking, and it is also a great introduction to making through-tenon keyed joints, one of the hallmarks of Arts & Crafts period furniture.

Early Craftsman pieces were fumed with ammonia to develop their characteristic color, but later pieces were stained and finished with early versions of modern stains and lacquer. In truth, there isn't much difference in appearance between the two types of finishes, and a more predictable and consistent finish can be achieved with stain. Predictability and consistency are the problems with fuming. Fuming depends on a chemical reaction between tannins in the wood and the ammonia, so variations in the chemical composition from one board to another lead to different colors.

If you fume, you'll likely need to touch something up with aniline dye, or layer on colored shellac to even out the color. It isn't that difficult to do, but it takes some patience and a practiced touch. The top coat used over the fumed oak also plays a big role in the final appearance. When you're finished fuming the wood is a dirty, greenish gray and the first time you do it, you will think you ruined it. Garnet or amber shellac make it a nice warm brown.

My favorite finishing method looks authentic and is easy to apply, but it takes a few days. Each step doesn't take too long, but each step needs to dry overnight. This isn't a "Christmas Eve" finish. As always, experiment on some scraps to get the color you want before committing the entire workpiece.

Prior to staining, I hand-sand everything with #150-grit Abranet. I use a pad that hooks up to a vacuum, but regular sandpaper also works. Quartersawn white oak takes stain well, but it is possible to make it too smooth and polished. When that happens, the stain just sits on top of the wood and won't color evenly. After sanding, I dampen the surfaces with distilled water, wait overnight, then sand again with #220-grit paper.

The first step is to stain the wood with an oil-based stain. Almost any stain with "walnut" in the name will come close to an authentic color. I look for something that is only a stain; if the label mentions "stain and finish in one," I choose something else. I flood on the stain, wait about 15 minutes, wipe off the excess and leave it to dry until the next day.

Following the stain, I apply one coat of Watco Danish Oil. There are different colors available, and again, the walnut tones give an

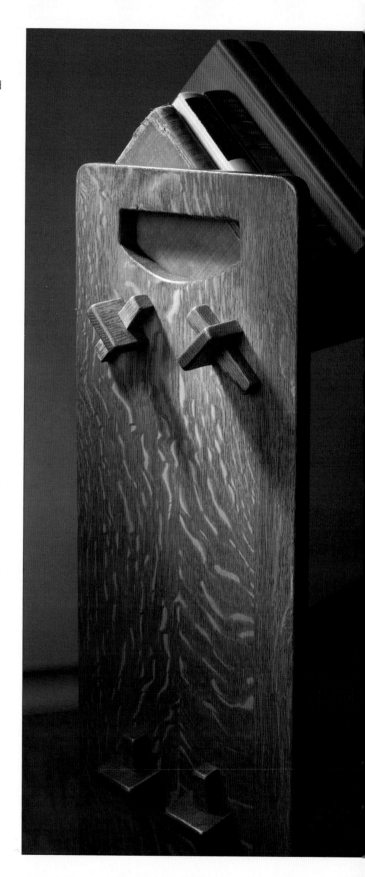

appropriate color. I flood the surface with oil, and use a synthetic steel wool pad to work it in. I let it soak in for 15 minutes, wipe dry and come back a day later.

The stain and the oil work together to highlight the wood figure with an even tone overall. In authentic Craftsman pieces, the grain doesn't "pop," that is, there isn't a drastic difference between the flakes and rays and the surrounding surface. I follow the oil with a coat or two of shellac.

Amber shellac for the first coat will warm up the color and give it an old look. I thin the shellac from the can, if it's a new can I use about half shellac, half denatured alcohol. If it's a can I've used before, it likely has had thinned shellac poured back into it, so I thin it less the next time. I use a good brush and judge how thin the shellac ought to be by how it feels as it goes on.

If you're concerned about durability, you can top coat the shellac with lacquer or varnish. I think shellac is more durable than a lot of people would have you believe, unless you're in the habit of sloshing alcohol around your furniture. I usually just apply paste wax – clear wax most of the time or the stinky dark wax if the color is a bit too light. If the shellac is too shiny, I'll take an abrasive pad to it before waxing, but most of the time I use the abrasive pad to apply the wax. After it dries I buff it with a cotton rag for a satin sheen.

# Harvey Ellis Bookcase

## A faithful reproduction of the epitome of Arts & Crafts design.

Gustav Stickley once wrote that the best way to learn furniture design was to build a proven design. He wrote that the student "learns from the start the fundamental principles of design and proportion and so comes naturally to understand what is meant by thorough workmanship." This bookcase is one of the finest examples of proportion and detail that make the Craftsman style more than just a simple piece of furniture.

In 1903 Harvey Ellis designed this glass-door bookcase while working as a designer for Stickley. The first time I saw an original example of this piece of furniture I was struck by how perfectly proportioned it was and how well all of the details combine.

These details also present some challenges in building. While this is a relatively simple piece, the joinery must be precisely executed. Before I began, I spent some time tuning up our table saw and jointer, made sure my squares and measuring tools were in order, and sharpened my chisels and planes.

We have the choice to work by hand, work by power or work with both. If we understand where each method excels – as well as where each falls short – we can master both sides and produce furniture we're proud of, without taking forever to make it.

## harvey ellis bookcase

| | NO. | ITEM | DIMENSIONS (INCHES) T | W | L | MATERIAL | COMMENTS |
|---|---|---|---|---|---|---|---|
| **CARCASE** | | | | | | | |
| ❑ | 1 | Top | 3/4 | 14 | 36 | Oak | |
| ❑ | 2 | Sides | 3/4 | 13 | 57 1/4 | Oak | |
| ❑ | 1 | Bottom | 3/4 | 13 | 31 1/2 | Oak | |
| ❑ | 1 | Bottom edge trim | 1/2 | 3/4 | 32 | Oak | |
| ❑ | 2 | Arched rails | 3/4 | 5 | 33 1/4 | Oak | 31" between tenons-tenons extend 3/8" past sides |
| ❑ | 2 | Face frame stiles | 7/8 | 1 1/2 | 50 1/2 | Oak | |
| ❑ | 1 | Face frame rail | 7/8 | 1 1/8 | 29 | Oak | 28" between tenons |
| ❑ | 2 | Applied pilasters | 1/4 | 1 | 50 1/2 | Oak | |
| ❑ | 2 | Capitals | 7/8 | 2 1/8 | 1 1/8 | Oak | |
| ❑ | 2 | Shelves | 3/4 | 11 1/8 | 30 7/8 | Oak | |
| **DOORS** | | | | | | | |
| ❑ | 2 | Stiles | 3/4 | 2 1/2 | 49 3/8 | Oak | Door opening is 28" x 49 3/8" |
| ❑ | 1 | Top rail | 3/4 | 2 1/2 | 24 1/2 | Oak | 23" between tenons |
| ❑ | 1 | Bottom rail | 3/4 | 3 1/2 | 24 1/2 | Oak | 23" between tenons |
| ❑ | 2 | Intermediate stiles | 3/4 | 1 1/4 | 44 3/8 | Oak tenons | 43 3/8" between |
| ❑ | 1 | Intermediate rail | 3/4 | 1 1/4 | 24 | Oak | 23" between tenons |
| ❑ | 3 | Top lights | 1/8 | 7 5/16 | 7 5/16 | Glass | |
| ❑ | 3 | Lower lights | 1/8 | 7 5/16 | 35 13/16 | Glass | |
| ❑ | 18 | Glass stops | 1/4 | 1/4 | 7 5/16 | Oak | |
| ❑ | 6 | Glass stops | 1/4 | 1/4 | 35 13/16 | Oak | |
| **BACK** | | | | | | | |
| ❑ | 2 | Stiles | 3/4 | 1 1/2 | 50 7/8 | Oak | |
| ❑ | 2 | Rails | 3/4 | 1 1/2 | 29 1/2 | Oak | 28 1/2" between tenons |
| ❑ | 1 | Mid rail | 3/4 | 2 | 29 1/2 | Oak | 28 1/2" between tenons |
| ❑ | 12 | Back panel slats | 1/4 | 4 7/8 | 23 7/16 | Oak | Shiplapped |

## True to the Original

Original Craftsman furniture was occasionally made in mahogany or figured maple, but the vast majority was made from quartersawn white oak. This method of sawing yields more stable material than plain sawn oak, and the distinctive rays can be absolutely stunning. White oak is much more of a furniture wood than red oak, giving a smoother and more refined appearance.

In addition to using this wood, I also decided to use the same method of finishing that was originally used, fuming the finished piece with ammonia, and using shellac followed by wax.

Tannic acid in the wood reacts with the fumes from the ammonia, yielding a distinctive coloration in the rays and flecks, as well as in the rest of the wood. Staining, glazing and dyeing can come close to the color of an original Stickley piece, but fuming can match it exactly.

I had to glue stock together to obtain the widths required. Because the final color was dependant on a chemical reaction, and the tannic acid content of white oak will vary from tree to tree and board to board, I was careful to match boards for color as well as for figure. I also cut

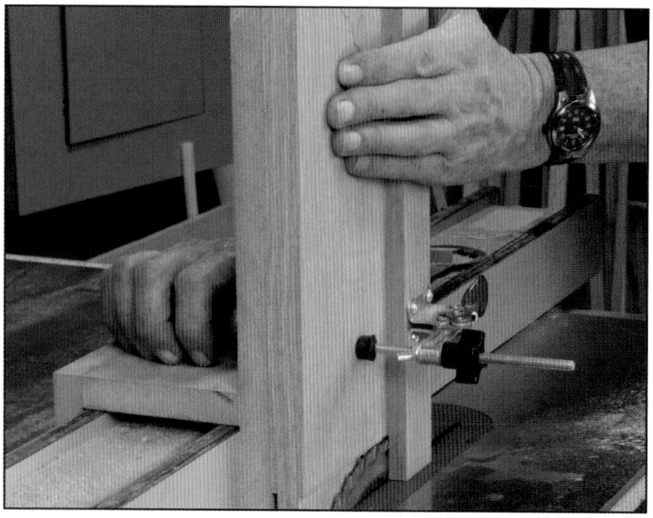

*The long mortises on the ends of the rails are cut with this tenoning jig that rides along the table saw fence.*

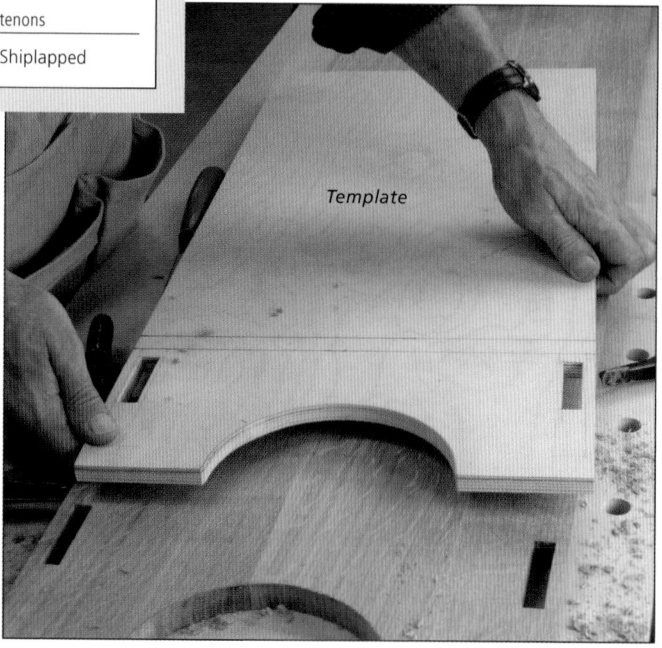


*The template locates the through mortises precisely, as well as the arched cutout and the location of the dado for the bottom of the case.*

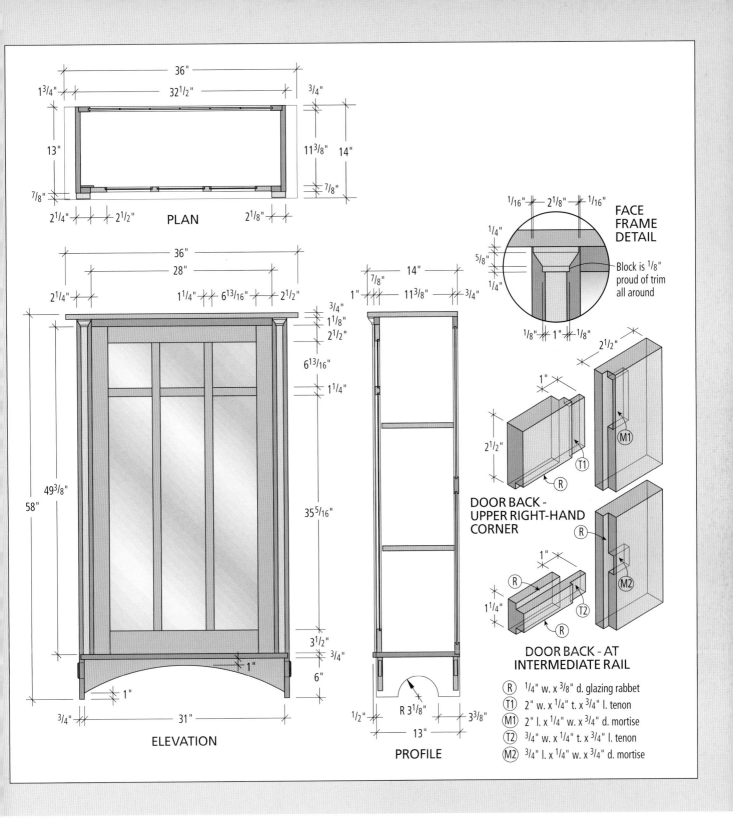

**PLAN**

**ELEVATION**

**PROFILE**

**FACE FRAME DETAIL**

Block is 1/8" proud of trim all around

**DOOR BACK - UPPER RIGHT-HAND CORNER**

**DOOR BACK - AT INTERMEDIATE RAIL**

(R) 1/4" w. x 3/8" d. glazing rabbet
(T1) 2" w. x 1/4" t. x 3/4" l. tenon
(M1) 2" l. x 1/4" w. x 3/4" d. mortise
(T2) 3/4" w. x 1/4" t. x 3/4" l. tenon
(M2) 3/4" l. x 1/4" w. x 3/4" d. mortise

most of the parts for the door from the same piece of wood so that the color would be as close as possible.

## Mortising With a Template

I began the joinery work with the through mortise-and-tenon joints at the bottom of the case sides. I made a template from 1/2"-thick plywood, which helped me locate the mortises and the arched cut-outs. I cut the mortises in the template with a

1/2"-diameter bit in my plunge router, guided by the router's fence, and squared the ends with a chisel and a rasp.

I could have used this same method on the actual cabinet sides, but by using the template I only had to do the layout work once, and if I slipped with the plunge router, the damage would be to a piece of plywood, not my finished end panel.

With the template clamped to the bottom of the end panel, I drilled most of the mortise with a 3/8" Forstner bit, and then used a router with a flush trim bit to trim the sides of the mor-

*After the tenons are trimmed to fit with a shoulder plane and scraper, the exposed ends are rounded with a block plane.*

*With the rails already glued to one stile, the shiplapped boards for the back panel are slipped into the groove in the rail. When they were all in place, I glued on the remaining stile.*

*To control glue squeeze-out on the exposed tenons, I get the tenon started in the mortise, then apply glue directly to the tenon.*

tises flush to the template. I used the smallest diameter flush trim bit I had to minimize the amount of material left in the corners. With the template still clamped to the panel, I used the edges of the mortise in the template to guide the chisel in the corners. A riffler and a flat rasp completed the work on the mortises.

## Dados and Rabbets

On the inside of the end panels there is a dado to hold the bottom and a rabbet from the top down to the dado to house the back. I made both of these cuts with a router and a ¾"-diameter straight bit. I used a shop-made T-square jig for the dado, and used the router's edge guide to make the rabbet, stopping at the dado for the bottom. I also ran a ¾"-wide by ¼"-deep rabbet along the back edge of the cabinet bottom.

With the work on the side panels complete, I turned to the tenons on the ends of the two arched rails that sit below the bottom and penetrate the sides.

I always like to "sneak up" on the fit of tenons, especially when they are exposed. The tricky part with through tenons is that the final cut that yields a good fit must also be smooth enough to give a good finish. I made the initial cuts on the table saw, using a jig that rides on the fence as shown.

With the bottom in place in its dado, I held the rails in place, and marked the locations of the top and bottom of the tenons directly from the mortises in the end panels. I made these cuts on the band saw, then I cleaned up all the saw marks with a shoulder plane. As I got close to a good fit, I switched to a card scraper. Once I had the tenons fitting nicely, I took a piece of ³⁄₃₂"-thick scrap, and placed it on the outside of the cabinet with its edge against the tenon. I then marked a pencil line around the tenons. This established a starting point for the rounded ends of the exposed tenons. I used my block plane and a rasp to bevel and round over the ends of the tenons, shown below.

*With the two bottom rails in place, I spread glue on the top edges of the rails and in the dado before tipping the bottom in to place.*

*After spreading glue on the end of the bottom, and the cheeks of the tenons, the remaining cabinet side is carefully put in place.*

After the tenons were complete, I marked the midpoint of the arch, and drove a finishing nail ⅛" below that point. I also made a mark ⅜" in from each end at the bottom edge of the rail. I then bent a ⅛"-thick strip of wood across these three points, and marked the curve with a pencil. The curves in the end panels had been marked from the template, and all of these cuts were made with my jigsaw.

The next task was to join the two stiles and top rail that make up the face frame of the carcase. I cut tenons on the end of the rail with a stack dado set in the table saw, and made the mortises at the top of the two stiles with a hollow chisel mortiser. I glued the rail between the stiles, and set this subassembly aside while I worked on the back panel.

*The trapezoid shaped block is laid out on each end of a long piece of wood to make cutting and handling easier.*

*Because of the mechanical fit of the rails and bottom, it only take a couple clamps to secure the bottom of the case assembly.*

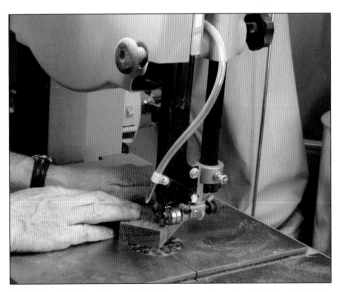

*All of the cuts to form the capital block were made on the band saw, as shown here. The final cut will be made after the block is smooth.*

*Leaving the block attached gives me plenty of material to clamp in the vise while I smooth out the saw marks with a rasp, followed by a file, and then #150-grit sandpaper.*

*Half-lap joints hold the intermediate stiles and rails of the doors together.*

## Panelled Back

Backs in original Craftsman pieces varied depending on when they were made, and could be V-grooved or shiplapped planks, or frame-and-panel assemblies. I chose to make a back panel, as this would help keep the cabinet from racking.

The stiles and rails for the back are all ¾"-thick material, with a ¼"-wide by ⅛"-deep groove centered in one edge. Mortise-and-tenon joints hold the panel together, and the ¼"-thick shiplapped panels float in the grooves in the stiles and rails. You also could use ¼"-thick plywood for the back panels, or make the entire back from one piece of ¾"- thick plywood.

To assemble the back, I first glued one end of each of the three rails into one of the stiles. After letting the glue dry overnight, I slipped the shiplapped panels into place, then applied glue to the tenons on the rails, and clamped on the remaining stile.

## Assembling the Case

With one of the end panels flat on the end of my assembly table, I inserted the tenons for the bottom rails part way in their mortises, and then applied glue to the tenons. This keeps the glue from squeezing out on the outside of the joint. I tapped the rails home with a dead-blow mallet, and then eased the bottom in to its dado, as shown at right. With these parts together, I put glue on the tenons of the rails, and edge of the bottom before clamping down the remaining side panel.

I then laid the cabinet on its back, and glued and clamped the face frame in place. After letting the glue dry for an hour, I glued the trim piece on the front edge of the bottom. The seam between the face frame and the end panel is covered by a ¼"-thick strip that runs from the top edge of the bottom to the bottom of the top face-frame rail.

These small additional pieces add interest to the design by creating steps in an otherwise flat surface. They also hide

*The half-lap joints, as well as all of the tenons for the door were cut with the dado head on the table saw as you can see here. The block clamped to the saw's fence locates the cuts without trapping the parts between the dado cutter and the fence.*

*I assemble the door in stages. Here I'm placing a subassembly of the intermediate stiles and rail to one of the door stiles. The remaining stile will be placed on top and clamped.*

After sanding all of the parts, I placed them in an airtight fuming tent, located by the back door of the shop.

*After "fuming" for 24 hours the tent was aired out and the plastic removed. Here you can see the construction of the tent frame, and the change in color.*

*The quartersawn white oak in its natural color.*

the joints and display quartersawn figure on the front of the cabinet.

I made a template out of ½"-thick baltic birch plywood that located the holes for the pegs that support the two adjustable shelves. After drilling the holes, the carcase was complete, except for the two blocks that cap the trim on the top front of the cabinet. I laid out the blocks on each end of a piece of wood about a foot long to give me room to hold them while cutting them on the band saw (shown bottom right).

This extra material also provided a way to hold the blocks in my bench vise while cleaning them up with a rasp. After all the surfaces were smooth, I glued them in place.

## Door

With the back panel completed, and the case parts assembled, It was time to work on the door. The glass sits in a ¼"-wide by ⅜"-deep rabbet and is held in place with ¼"-square strips of wood. This glass stop is nailed in place after the cabinet is finished. The outer stiles and rails are held together with mortise-and-tenon joints. The intermediate stiles and rail also have tenons on their ends. The door tenons all have a step in them to accommodate the

rabbet for the door's glass. The ¼"-wide mortises are in line with the inside of the rabbet.

At the upper portion of the bookcase door, the intermediate rail joins the two narrow stiles with a half-lap joint as shown on page 86. I made the joints for the outer stiles and rails, and then clamped the door together to lay out the joints for the intermediate stiles and rails. I cut these joints, as well as the all tenons for all the door parts, with a stack dado set in the table saw.

I assembled the door in stages, to avoid putting together a lot of parts at once. I assembled the half-lap joints first. The top and bottom rails were then put on the ends of the smaller stiles and clamped. While this assembly was drying, I cut the mortise for the lock, and carved the recess to inlay the brass escutcheon for the keyhole.

I secured one of the long stiles in my bench vise (as shown below), and put glue in the mortises before placing the tenons of the rail assembly. Next I put some glue on the top edges of the tenons on the rails. Then I tapped the second rail in place before I began clamping.

## Fumed Finish

Fuming white oak with ammonia is an exercise in faith; the color doesn't look right until the piece is finished with shellac and dark wax. There is also a distinct risk that some parts won't come out the same color as others, or, perhaps worse, that there will be some sapwood present that won't take on any color at all.

Twenty-six percent ammonia is used in blue print machines, and is a much stronger solution than household ammonia, which is about five percent. Such a strong chemical requires great care in handling, as the fumes can quickly damage eyes,

*After exposure to ammonia fumes for 24 hours, the oak has turned a grayish brown color.*

*Garnet shellac adds some color, and highlights the distinctive grain. Dark wax will complete the finish.*

skin and lungs. Make sure to where gloves, goggles and a respirator when handling it. I also took steps to minimize the time that the ammonia was exposed to the environment in our shop.

Before fuming the entire piece, I did some tests on scraps. As I worked on this project, I saved the cutoff pieces from the end panels and top. I put these, along with other scraps in a plastic container with an airtight lid. I put some ammonia in a small plastic bowl in the larger container, sealed the lid, and let this sit for 24 hours. Satisfied that the final result would be close to matching, I built a frame from inexpensive 1 by 3 pine and covered it with 4-mil-thick plastic sheet, as shown at right.

I tucked the plastic under the wood frame at the floor, and secured it to the frame with spring clamps to get an airtight seal. I left one end open so that I could place the assembled cabinet and all of the parts inside. Once everything to be fumed was inside, I clamped most of the opening closed, leaving just enough room at the bottom to reach in and pour the ammonia in to a plastic container. After this, I sealed the rest of the end and waited a day.

When it came time to remove the cabinet from the tent, I put on my goggles, gloves and respirator, opened the bottom of the end, and put a lid on the plastic container inside. I then put a fan in the opening, and exhausted the fumes outside. After letting the fan run for an hour, I opened the tent completely.

Most of the pieces came out close in color, but there were a few parts that were a bit lighter, and a couple edges that didn't take at all. Overall though, I was happy with the results, and prepared to deal with the inconsistencies.

The first step after fuming was to smooth all of the surfaces with a nylon abrasive (Scotchbrite) pad, and give everything

two coats of garnet shellac, in a two-pound cut. I then mixed some aniline dye (Liberon Fumed Oak light) with some alcohol. With a 1"-wide sash brush, I applied the dye to the lighter areas, brushing on slight amounts until the color was close. I followed this with two more coats of shellac.

The shellac changes the dirty-looking brownish gray of the fumed oak to warm brown. The photos at right show the progression of the color from raw wood, fuming and shellac. The color from the shellac, however, is just a bit too orange, and needs to be waxed to achieve the desired rich brown I was looking for. I smoothed all the surfaces with #320-grit sandpaper, followed by a Scotchbrite pad.

The final step in finishing was to apply dark paste wax, which fills the open pores of the oak, and tones down the color from the garnet shellac, leaving the piece a rich warm brown.

With the finish complete, I installed the glass in the door, holding it in place with ¼" x ¼" glass stop. I mitered the corners, and attached the stop to the inside of the openings with 23 gauge pins.

All that remained was to install the lock and escutcheon in the door, hang the door and attach the top with figure-8 fasteners. I placed three fasteners in the front and back rails, and one in the center of each of the end panels.

Harvey Ellis's association with Gustav Stickley lasted only a few months before Ellis died in January 1904. Ellis's influence on Arts and Crafts design however was tremendous. The details he produced for Stickley have served as hallmarks of the period.

Ellis related the arrangement of spaces in good design to the notes in a musical chord. This bookcase combines the practical and architectural elements that he is known for in perfect harmony, and serves as a fitting tribute to his genius.

# Tusk Tenon Bookrack

## Hand and power tools work together to make signature Arts & Crafts joints.

The dividing line between hand-tool woodworking and machine-tool woodworking doesn't exist for me. Although I'm not fond of noise and dust, I have an appreciation for what machines can do – make work faster and repeatable. I also know there are times when the right tool for the job is powered by what my grandfather called elbow grease.

This small bookrack can be made entirely by using hand tools, or entirely by using machines. I used both, and as we go through the steps of making it, you will find out why.

The key elements in this project are the through tenons that connect the shelf to the ends. I based the design on an early 20th century example from the Roycroft community. It's an ideal way to learn this method of joinery – it only takes a few board feet of material and each of the steps is an opportunity to improve your skills.

A project like this is enjoyable if the parts go together with a minimum amount of fuss. That means that the mortises and tenons need to be in the right places, and at the right sizes.

I used a pair of templates and a router with a flush-trimming bit to locate and size the joints. This way, the work of getting things to fit has to be done only once, when making the templates. Work on the real parts goes quickly and if I want to make this piece again, or make a batch of them, I'm well on my way before I even begin building.

*Machine precision, hand-worked details. This bookrack features tusk tenons. Blended techniques make it simple to build.*

*Form and function. The first template generates the shape of the ends and the through mortises. The oak blank below it is cut 1/16" oversize, and the holes minimize the work for the router bit.*

*Guided by the kerf. One precise cut establishes the size of the tenon. This L-shaped jig attached to the miter gauge is simple and safe.*

The patterns are made from ½" Baltic birch plywood. MDF would also work, but the plywood's edges hold up better over time. You can enlarge the drawing on page 93 or you can download a full-size version on our web site *popularwood-working.com/aug07 online extras* and print it yourself. Before cutting the outer shape, lay out and make the mortises.

There are many possible ways to make the mortises. I used a ⅝"-diameter straight bit in a plunge router, guided by the router's fence. With the pattern blank firmly clamped to my bench I plunged the router within my layout lines to make the cut.

## Make the Templates

The advantage of the router is that it removes a lot of material quickly, making smooth mortises with parallel sides. The disadvantage is that it can't make a mortise with square ends. But two hand tools – the chisel and the rasp – solve this problem quickly. First on the template and then on the real parts.

Because I had to square the rounded ends of the mortise slots by hand, I didn't bother setting any stops for the ends of the mortises. I did it by eye, starting and stopping about ¹⁄₁₆" inside the lines.

After chopping away most of the waste in the corners with the chisel, finish the mortises with a rasp. With those done, cut the outer shape of the pattern with the band saw or jigsaw, and smooth the perimeter with the rasp before adding the stops as seen in the photo above. A dab of glue and a couple 23-gauge pins hold the stops in place.

The shelf template is made from the template for the ends. Line up one edge of the shelf pattern blank to the end of one of the mortises in the other template and transfer mortise locations. The ⅜" offset in the shelf pattern allows space for the edge that will be added to the back of the shelf after the bookrack is assembled.

Make the cuts that define the edges of the tenons on the table saw, as seen in the photo above. To do this, screw a couple pieces

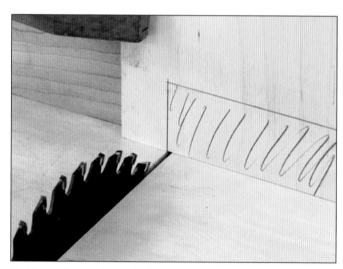

*Nothing to chance. The saw kerf in the horizontal part of the jig shows exactly where the blade will cut. With the layout line at the kerf line, clamp the piece to the jig.*

of scrap together in an "L" shape and attach that to the miter gauge of the table saw. This provides a reference for where the blade will be during the cut.

Clamp the shelf pattern to the miter gauge attachment to hold it in position and to keep your hands a safe distance from the blade during the cut.

To remove the waste between the tenons, make a rough cut on the waste side of the layout lines at the band saw then clamp a straight piece of plywood directly on the line. Then, with a flush-cutting bit in a router, trim the pattern back to the line and clean up the corners with a chisel. The goal at this point is to get the tenons on the shelf pattern to fit in width in the mortises of the end pattern, as seen at right.

When pattern-trimming mortises in solid wood parts like this, I always use the smallest diameter router bit available. This mini-mizes the curved waste left in the inside corners. I use the patterns to trace the shapes on the wood. I keep close to, but just outside the lines to reduce the material the router will remove. Then I cut all the parts to rough sizes.

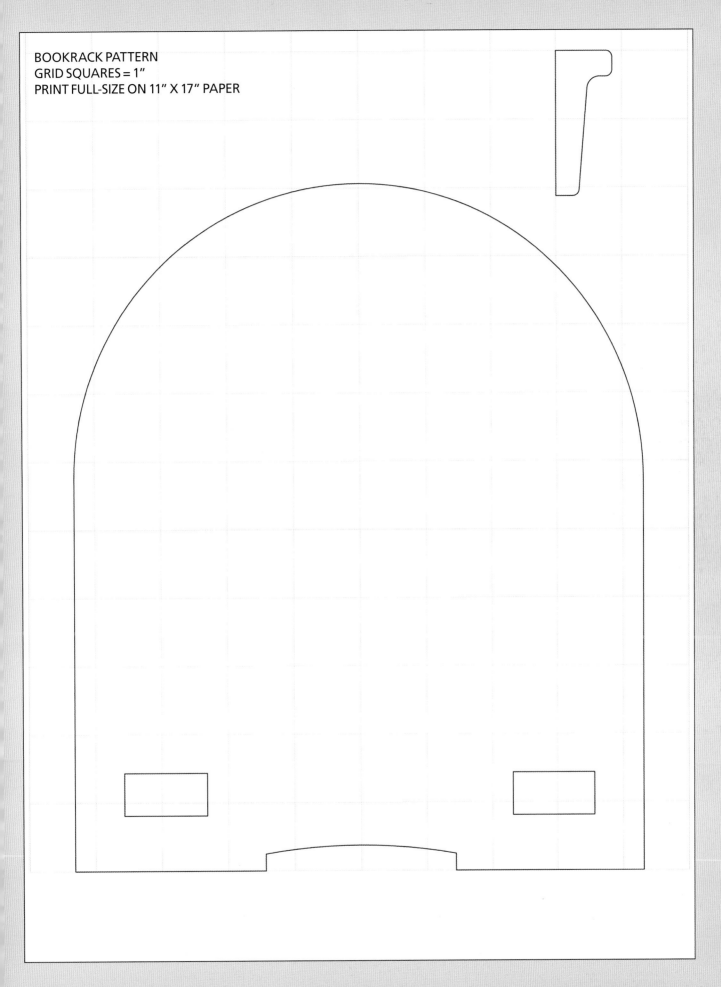

BOOKRACK PATTERN
GRID SQUARES = 1"
PRINT FULL-SIZE ON 11" X 17" PAPER

Get this right and success will follow. Take time to fit the tenons in the shelf template to the mortises in the end pattern. When the parts are routed to the templates, the joints will work.

Built-in guidance system. The flat area of the routed mortise acts as a guide for the back of the chisel. Rest the back against the cut and swing the edge of the chisel down to the corner (above). This shallow line will guide the tool in the next step of making the cut. With the edge of the chisel in the line, push straight down. Clean up both end-grain surfaces of the mortise and then finish the cut on the ends. The long-grain cuts tend to split, so shave off a little at a time (right). A few strokes with a rasp will finish the mortises.

## Good Reason to Go Backward

Hogging off a lot of solid wood is an invitation to chipping or tearing out the solid wood, particularly on the curves. Clamp the patterns and the parts securely to your bench and make the first pass moving the router counterclockwise around the outside of the pattern. Climb cutting in this way helps to reduce chipping and tear-out. Drill two holes at the mortise locations to allow the bearing on the bit to reach the pattern below.

After routing the mortises, the corners have to be squared. I use a chisel and put the back against the end-grain edge of the straight part of the mortise. Holding the chisel flush, swing the corner down to establish a straight line.

Turn the chisel 90° to set the perpendicular line at the end of the mortise. Then, go back to the end-grain side and force the chisel down as far as possible, cutting across the grain. After cutting the two opposite end-grain faces, make paring cuts with the grain.

The tenons will fit in the width of the mortise – or at least be very close – from the template. To get them to fit in thickness, and to establish a shoulder on the inside of the joint, trim half the difference in thickness off each cheek of the tenon, using the jig shown in the photo above right.

Before fitting the tenons, chamfer the ends. This makes starting the tenons in the mortises easier, and it prevents the tenon from doing any damage on the way out of the other side of the mortise. Start the ends in the mortises and push down. If they stop, look to see which face of the tenon should be trimmed.

## Tight But Not Too Tight

Aim for a snug fit. It's right when you can force the first part of the tenon into the mortise by hand, and are able to lift both pieces without the joint coming apart. Take a few licks with a card scraper or rasp to remove the saw and router marks from the tenon.

This loosens the joint just enough to get it almost all the way home with hand pressure. A few taps with a dead-blow mallet seats the shoulder of the joint. Mark a pencil line where the cheek of the tenon meets the face of the end piece. After all the work of putting the joint together, it's time to take it apart again to make the small mortises for the tusks.

The tusks pull the tenon into the mortise by bearing on the face of the mortised end. Locating the back of the mortise just behind the face ensures this. After offsetting the pencil line on the tenon $1/16$" back, mark out a square, centered mortise and cut it with one stroke of a $1/2$" chisel on the hollow-chisel mortiser. A block of scrap under the tenon holds it above the machine's table and prevents the back side from tearing out as the chisel exits. This mortise could, of course, be made by

# Keyed-tenon Bookrack

| NO. | ITEM | DIMENSIONS (INCHES) | | | MATERIAL | COMMENTS |
|---|---|---|---|---|---|---|
| | | T | W | L | | |
| ❑ 2 | Ends | 3/4 | 8 5/8 | 10 1/8 | QSWO | Cut big, rout to size |
| ❑ 1 | Shelf | 3/4 | 7 1/2 | 20 | QSWO | |
| ❑ 4 | Keys | 1/2 | 7/8 | 2 1/8 | QSWO | Cut from longer piece |
| ❑ 1 | Shelf edge | 3/8 | 1 1/4 | 16 1/2 | QSWO | |

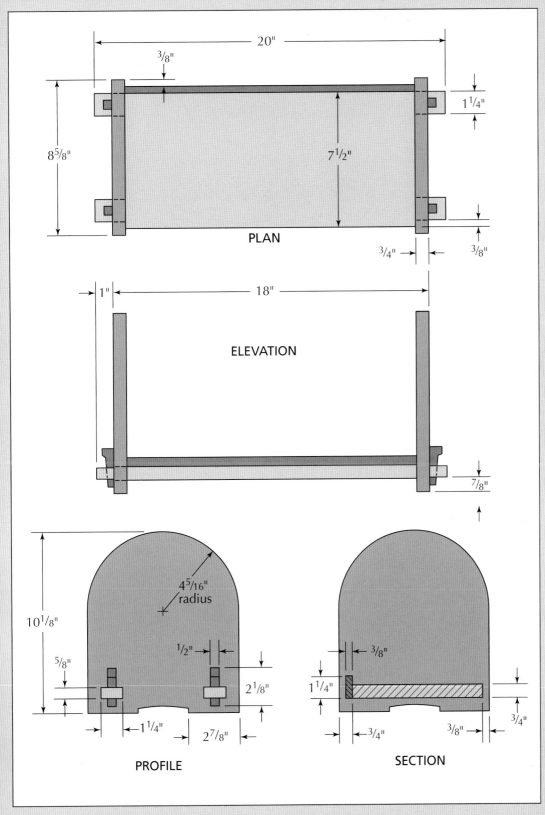

PLAN

ELEVATION

PROFILE

SECTION

*Cutting the shoulders. Use the tenoning jig to make the shoulder cuts on the through tenons. The clamp on the far end holds the workpiece to the jig.*

*Insurance before fitting. Chamfering the ends of the through tenons before fitting them makes them easier to start in the mortises and prevents damage on the way out of the other side.*

*Eyeing the angle. Set the chisel on the line and lean the chisel back until the edge is in line with the bottom of the mortise. Strike the chisel with a mallet to complete the cut.*

*Just a bit behind. The back edge of the second through mortise is back from the face of the end 1/16". The tusk will then be able to pull the joint tight.*

drilling a ³⁄₈" or ⁷⁄₁₆" hole and squaring the corners with a chisel if a mortising machine isn't available.

## Taking Aim on the Angle

The outer edge of the mortise is sloped about ¹⁄₁₆" in the thickness of the tenon to match the angle on the tusks. This wedging action locks the joint together and if the tusks loosens from wood shrinkage, gravity or a tap on top will tighten the joint.

Holding the back of the chisel against the long-grain sides of the small mortise, swing the edge of the chisel down to nick the corners at the layout line.

Then, place the edge of the chisel on the line and push straight down. Don't push hard – just enough to make an incision along the pencil line. The edge of the chisel will fit in this slit; tilt the handle of the chisel toward you. Looking down the handle, aim for the edge at the bottom of the mortise. With the chisel in position, a few taps with a mallet make the slanted cut on the inside of the mortise.

To make the tusks, mill some scrap slightly thicker than the ¹⁄₂" mortise and about ⁷⁄₈" wide. Make lengths that are roughly two tusks long plus 1", and plane the tusks until they fit the mortise in width. Lay out two tusks, cut them to shape on the band saw then drive one end into the mortise.

The excess length on the tusks gives some room to fiddle with the fit of the angled tusks in the slanted mortise. A rasp followed by a card scraper removes the band-saw marks on the tusks. When the fit is good, mark the bottom of the tusks ¹⁄₄" up from the bottom of the end and ³⁄₄" above the top cheek of the tenon.

Then mark the final outline of the tusks, trim them with the band saw and finish shaping with a rasp. When all four tusks fit, take the entire piece apart one last time to scrape and sand the surfaces. Sand the wide surfaces and exposed edges, but stay away from the through tenons and parts of the tusks that fit in the small mortises.

## To Glue or Not to Glue

The original version of the bookrack was shipped in a flat carton, and assembled by the purchaser. Glue is an option, but not a necessity, to hold the tusk joints together. I don't bother with it – the joints are surprisingly strong on their own.

After final assembly, the exposed parts of the tenons and tusks are scraped and sanded. While quartersawn white oak is tough to cut, it is easy to sand. I generally go over the entire piece with a card scraper and only sand with #150 or #180 grit.

The back edge of the shelf is the last piece attached. After cutting it to size and sanding it, run a bead of glue along the edge of the shelf, and hold the edge to the shelf with a few clamps, then let the glue dry overnight. The next morning, off go the clamps and on goes the finish.

I usually put a darker finish on pieces like this, but every now and then I like to see a piece without any added color. On this shelf, I used two coats of amber shellac. After letting the shellac dry thoroughly, scuff it with a Scotch-Brite pad and apply a coat of paste wax.

# Greene & Greene Sideboard

Authentic details are easier than you think.

In 1907, the architectural practice of brothers Charles and Henry Greene was at its peak of popularity in southern California, with several houses under construction. Equally busy was the workshop of Peter and John Hall, another pair of brothers who were responsible for the actual construction of the ultimate bungalows designed by Greene and Greene.

In addition to acting as general contractors, the Halls were also responsible for all of the interior woodwork and the furniture for these magnificent homes. In researching this piece, I tried to discover what the original details were, and also tried to place myself in the setting in which the original work was done. Given the volume of work performed in the Halls' millwork shop, this furniture must have been made as efficiently as possible.

The original version of this serving table was made from mahogany with ebony accents for the Freeman Ford home in Pasadena, California. My version is about 12" shorter than the original and about 6" narrower. In planning this project, I wanted to come as close as I could to the details of the original piece. I found an amazing online resource for original Greene and Greene drawings and photographs. See "The Greene & Greene Virtual Archives" on page 103 for more information.

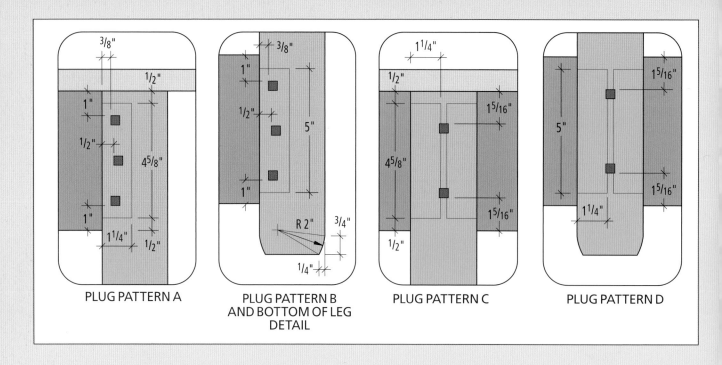

PLUG PATTERN A

PLUG PATTERN B
AND BOTTOM OF LEG
DETAIL

PLUG PATTERN C

PLUG PATTERN D

## Digging for the Details

In many Greene and Greene reproductions, the finished project doesn't look quite right, or the methods used are terribly inefficient. In highly detailed projects like this, half the battle is making nice details quickly. The other half is the sequence in which the work is performed.

Many times people follow someone else's reproduction, rather than referring to an original example. The problem with this is that details get changed or exaggerated, and then are taken as good examples. The style gets watered down and the methods become too complicated. I wanted to make this piece as it would have been made by the Hall brothers; excellent workmanship

done efficiently, faithful to the design.

I also wanted the color and character of the mahogany to look the way original pieces do. It took some detective work and head scratching to work out the methods and materials. In the end, this table looks more like the original than most reproductions.

My plans called for 32 mortise-and-tenon joints and 72 square plugs. The plugs on the legs appear to be going through the mortise-and-tenon joints that connect the rails to the legs. If you look closely at the inner set of legs on the previous page, you will notice that the plugs are centered in the width of the legs.

The only way these plugs could be functional would be if the tenons were long enough to cross the midpoint of the leg. If that were true, then the tenons would need to be reduced in thickness, so that they could cross each other. This would complicate these joints as well as weaken them. This set of plugs is just for show.

I also questioned the need for pinning all three of the plugs at each of the corner joints. One would be sufficient to reinforce the joint. Pinning all of them could weaken the tenons, and introduce problems when the rails expand and contract seasonally. I decided to pin only the middle of each tenon and make most of the plugs only decorative.

The original drawings detailed

## greene and greene sideboard

| | NO. | ITEM | DIMENSIONS (INCHES) | | | MATERIAL | COMMENTS |
|---|---|---|---|---|---|---|---|
| | | | T | W | L | | |
| ❏ | 1 | Top | 7/8 | 18 | 69 3/4 | Mahogany | 1/4" x 3/8" tongue each end |
| ❏ | 2 | Breadboard ends | 1 | 3 | 18 1/4 | Mahogany | 1/4" x 3/8" groove one edge, 1/4" x 5/8" x 2" groove both ends |
| ❏ | 8 | Legs | 2 3/4 | 2 3/4 | 29 1/8 | Mahogany | |
| ❏ | 2 | Top end rails | 7/8 | 5 5/8 | 13 | Mahogany | 1/2" x 1 1/4" x 4 5/8" tenon each end |
| ❏ | 2 | Lower end rails | 7/8 | 6 | 13 | Mahogany | 1/2" x 1 1/4" x 5" tenon each end |
| ❏ | 4 | F & B top rails | 7/8 | 5 5/8 | 8 1/4 | Mahogany | 1/2" x 1 1/4" x 4 5/8" tenon each end |
| ❏ | 2 | F & B cloud lift rails | 7/8 | 6 3/8 | 21 1/2 | Mahogany | 1/2" x 1 1/4" x 4 5/8" tenon each end |
| ❏ | 4 | F & B bottom rails | 7/8 | 6 | 8 1/4 | Mahogany | 1/2" x 1 1/4" x 5" tenon each end |
| ❏ | 2 | F & B bottom mid rails | 7/8 | 6 | 21 1/2 | Mahogany | 1/2" x 1 1/4" x 5" tenon each end |
| ❏ | 72 | Plugs | 3/8 | 3/8 | 5/16 | Walnut | Ebonized |
| ❏ | 4 | Splines | 1/4 | 7/8 | 6 | Walnut | Ebonized |
| ❏ | 2 | Cleats | 7/8 | 7/8 | 10 3/8 | Mahogany | |
| ❏ | 2 | Cleats | 7/8 | 7/8 | 18 7/8 | Mahogany | |

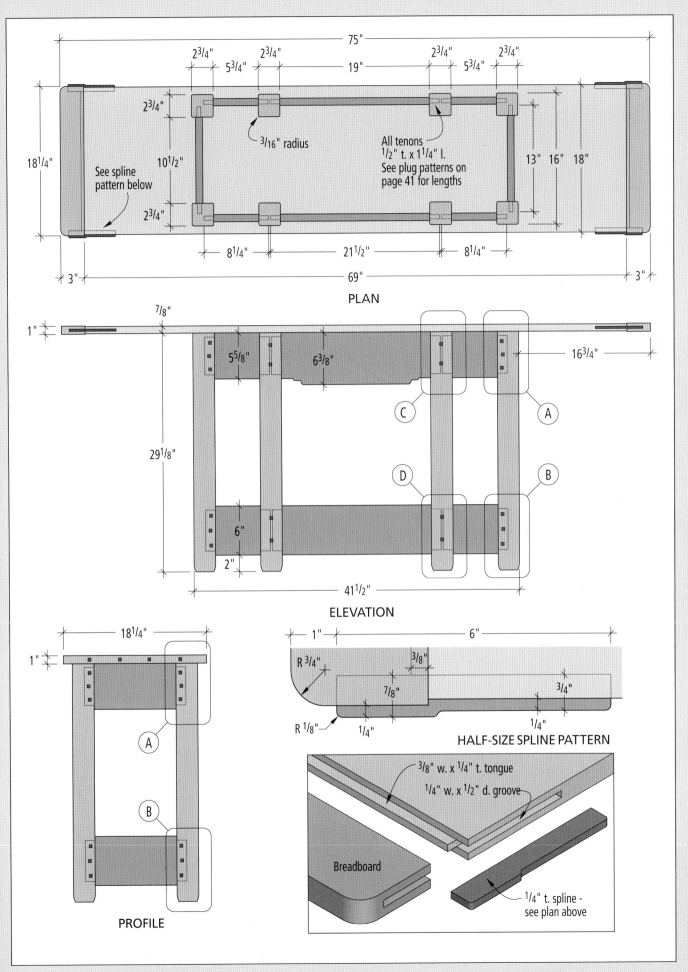

PLAN

2¾"
5¾"
2¾"
19"
2¾"
5¾"
2¾"
75"

2¾"
3/16" radius
All tenons
½" t. x 1¼" l.
See plug patterns on
page 41 for lengths

18¼"
10½"
13"  16"  18"

See spline
pattern below

2¾"
8¼"
21½"
8¼"

3"
69"
3"

ELEVATION

7/8"
1"
5⅝"
6⅜"
16¾"

C
A

D
B

29⅛"

6"
2"
41½"

PROFILE

18¼"
1"
A
B

HALF-SIZE SPLINE PATTERN

1"
6"
R ¾"
3/8"
7/8"
¾"
R ⅛"
¼"
¼"

3/8" w. x ¼" t. tongue
¼" w. x ½" d. groove

Breadboard

¼" t. spline -
see plan above

TABLES & CHAIRS 101

the breadboard ends, the splines and the way they are attached with screws behind the plugs.

Our local wood supplier had 3"-square by 30"-long leg blanks in stock, so I decided to purchase eight of them instead of milling my own out of 12/4 material. You might need to glue up the leg blanks from two or more pieces to get the thickness of 2¾".

The rest of the material all has a finished thickness of ⅞" except for the breadboard ends, which are a full 1" thick. I had wood that was long enough to make all of the top rails out of one piece and all of the bottom rails out of the other. I kept them in order to match grain and color around the entire table, which adds a nice touch.

## Which Leg is Which?

After laying out all of the legs and rails for grain direction and orientation, I numbered each leg on the plan view of my drawing, and wrote the number on the top of each leg to keep them in order as the work progressed. I also marked each end of the rails with the number of the leg it joined to.

My first task was to find an efficient way to cut all the mortises. Instead of using a hollow chisel mortiser, I decided to use a plunge router along with a template to quickly locate all of the cuts.

## More Mortises per Hour

The fence for the plunge router was used to locate the distance in from the edge of the leg to the mortises. In order to set the beginning and end of each mortise, I added a sub-base to the router as shown below, and attached a ½"-square block of wood to the sub-base. This size block matched the diameter of the bit I was using. I placed it in line with the router bit

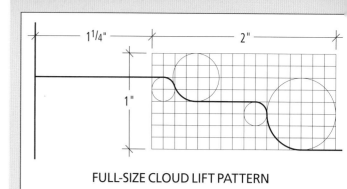

FULL-SIZE CLOUD LIFT PATTERN

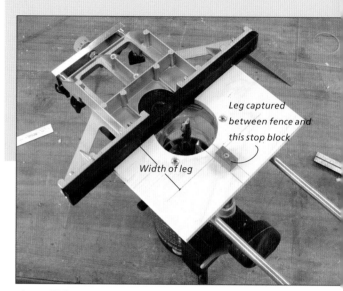

Leg captured between fence and this stop block

Width of leg

*The small block on the sub-base is the same size as the bit, placed farther away than the width of the leg from the fence.*

and square to the fence. The template was made to the exact length of the leg, with the notches cut at the end points of each mortise. After the notches were cut, I added a stop to locate the template at the top of each leg.

I took the four outer legs, and with a lumber crayon, marked the general location of the mortises on adjacent corners. I marked the four inner legs on opposite sides. These marks were to keep straight which surfaces were to be mortised. The exact locations of the mortises would come from the template without my needing to locate and mark each one.

I put each leg, along with the template in my bench vise, with the surface to be mortised facing up. I then routed the mortises, plunging back and forth until I reached the final depth of 1¼".

I cut all of the tenons on the rails with a jig on the table saw, coming in 3/16" from each face and ½" from each edge to form the tenons. I used a rasp to round off each of the tenon shoulders to match the rounded ends of the mortises I routed earlier.

To make the cloud lift patterns on the center rails, I made a template out of ½"-thick plywood, carefully filing the inside and outside curves at the corners. I then rough cut each of the cloud lifts with the band saw, and used the template and a ¼"-diameter flush trimming bit in the router to cut each rail to the pattern.

I fit each of the tenons, trimming with my shoulder plane, and then made a dry run assembly of the entire base of the table.

Block

Stop

*The block is lined up with the bit so that the template can be made to the exact size and location of the mortises.*

## The Greene & Greene Virtual Archives

The University of Southern California hosts an amazing online collection of original drawings, photographs, correspondence and other documents from the work of Charles Sumner Greene and Henry Mather Greene. You can find it online at: *usc.edu/dept/architecture/greeneandgreene/index.html*.

The database of digital images can be searched by project name or by type of object. Once a document has been found, you can zoom in and pan around on individual drawings and photographs. Background information and other reference material is also available.

I was able to find an original black and white photograph of the table featured in this article, and while drawings for this table don't exist, I looked at working drawings for other furniture from the same house, as well as a finish formula from the William Thorsen house.

This material served as the basis for how I made the details of this table. The shape and projection of the square plugs and splines on the breadboard ends, the treatment of the edges of the legs and top, and the finish color were all completed by following the details shown in these original documents.

## Productive Method for Plugs

With 64 square plugs to make for the table base, I didn't want to lay out the location of every hole. So I made a template the width and height of the legs and marked out the center points of each of the plugs, drilling a ⅛"-diameter hole at each of these points. I marked all of the legs by sticking my awl through each hole and into the face of the leg.

With a ⅜"-diameter Forstner bit in my drill press, set to bore ¼" deep, I drilled a hole for each of the square plugs. I could have made these holes with the mortiser, but with some of the squares offset ⅛" from the others, I didn't want to set up the mortiser fence three times. With the center points marked from the template, I saved time.

To make the holes square, I took a worn out ⅜" chisel from the mortiser, ground the points off the end, and with a conical bit in a Dremel tool, sharpened the back of each corner of the chisel. I clamped a scrap of plywood to the face of each leg with its edge tangent to each row of holes as shown below right. This kept the chisel square to the edge of the legs, and with a few smacks of the hammer the round holes were now square. I could have used a standard chisel and made four cuts on each hole, but this would have taken four times as long.

The bottoms of the legs were radiused with a 2"-radius round-over bit. I set up the bit in the router table, so that the radius ended ¾" up from the bottom of each leg and ¼" in. Using a thick block of wood to back up the legs, I moved each edge of the leg bottoms across the bit as seen on page 105.

Before finish sanding all the parts to #220 grit, I used a roundover bit in my router to ease all of the edges to a ³⁄₁₆" radius on the legs, and a ⅛" radius on the rails and edges of the tabletop.

## Not Ebony, but Ebonized

In original Greene and Greene furniture the square plugs were made of ebony, but I decided to use walnut, ebonizing them with

*With the template and the leg held in the vise, the fence on the router places the cut laterally, and the block hits the template to locate the ends of the mortises. Using this method allowed me to mill all 32 mortises quickly and precisely, without doing any layout work on the legs.*

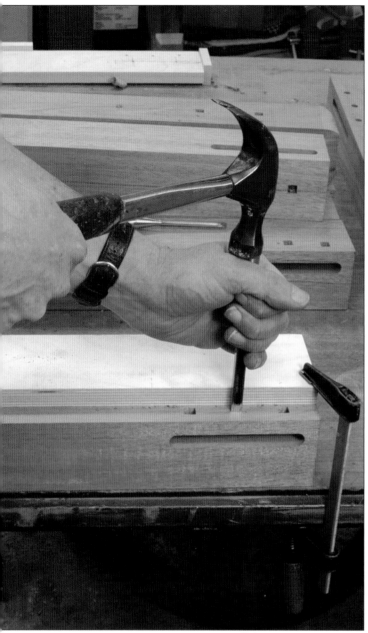

A modified chisel from a hollow chisel mortiser turns round holes square with just a few hammer taps. Plywood clamped to the leg keeps the chisel straight.

A small-diameter flush-cutting bit follows the template and shapes all of the cloud lifts accurately and identically leaving only minimal sanding to be done.

The tenons are adjusted to fit with my shoulder plane. A piece of scrap plywood attached to the bench acts as a bench stop to hold the work .

a solution made from vinegar and steel wool. I took a pint of white vinegar and dropped in a shredded pad of steel wool. After letting this soak for several days, I strained the liquid through a coffee filter to remove any metal.

Because I would be coloring the legs and the plugs separately, I wanted to shape the plugs and cut them to finished length before putting them in place.

To make the plugs, I ripped strips about 1/64" over the size of the 3/8" square holes. Using the miter gauge on the band saw I cut 1" long blocks. These were long enough to round over and bevel the ends before cutting them to final length. I put a slight dome and bevel on each end of the 1"-long blocks with a quarter-sheet pad sander, and set up a stop block on the miter gauge for the band saw 5/16" away from the blade. Carefully

holding the blocks against the miter gauge with the point of an awl, I cut them to length.

The last step was to put a small chamfer on each of the back edges with a chisel. The chamfer let me get the plugs started in the holes before driving them in with a dead-blow mallet.

The top was glued up from three 1"-thick boards, and after surfacing it to 7/8", I trimmed it to length. Each end of the top has a 1/4"-wide by 7/8"-long tongue to hold the breadboard ends. I clamped a piece of plywood across the top to serve as a straightedge for the router to mill the tongues, as shown above right.

I used a 1/4" straight bit in the router table to cut the groove in the center of one edge of the 1"-thick end pieces. I then raised the bit to 2" above the table to cut the 5/8"-deep slot in the end

Just a portion of a 2"-radius roundover bit shapes the bottoms of the legs.

*A piece of plywood clamped across the top guides the router to cut the tongue for the breadboard ends.*

The breadboard end is attached to the tabletop with screws and the ebonized walnut spline is glued in the slot in the table only.

of the breadboard to receive the splines. The last slot to cut was in the top for the other end of the splines. This was made with a slot-cutting bit in my hand-held router.

I made the first spline, and I used it as a pattern for the remaining three. I cut the splines a little oversized on the band saw and then fixed them to the pattern with double-sided tape. I used the flush-trim bit in the router to make exact copies of the splines. With a little sanding on the edges, and a few strokes of my block plane to adjust the thickness, the splines were ready to be ebonized.

The breadboard ends are held to the ends of the tabletop with #8 x 3½" screws. I drilled oversized holes through the ends, and moved the bit side to side in the two outer holes to elongate them. With glue applied only to the middle 6" of the tongue, I put the ends in place, temporarily inserted the splines to align the breadboard ends and tightened the screws.

## Authentic Color Uncovered

One of the most interesting discoveries I made on the Greene and Greene Virtual Archives was a recipe for the finish for the furniture from another house. I have always admired the rich,

vibrant color of the mahogany in original Greene and Greene furniture, something rarely seen in most reproductions of their work.

The formula called for a treatment of potassium dichromate applied "as work proceeds" followed by a "filler" composed of four colors mixed in linseed oil. Potassium dichromate is a powerful oxidizer and must be handled carefully. I wore a respirator while mixing it and gloves while applying it. After experimenting, I used a solution of ⅜ ounce of powder to a quart of distilled water.

For the colors, I used artist's oil colors. Chrome Yellow (3½ parts of the formula) and Raw Umber (3 parts) were easy selections. White Lead (2⅝ parts) is no longer made, so I used Titanium White. The last color listed was Sylvan Green (⅛ part), and I couldn't find an oil color with this name. Because it was a small part of the original mixture, I took a guess and used Hooker's Green.

I squeezed out the colors in the proportions given on a scrap of plywood and mixed them together with a pint of Danish oil. Following a recipe, I hadn't thought about what color would be the result. I was expecting a rich, reddish brown and was surprised to see a shade of green I haven't seen since my son has been out of diapers.

I was ready to abandon the experiment because of the horrendous color I had mixed, but curiosity won and I tried it on my sample board. After wiping off the excess, I was pleased to find a truly wonderful color and sheen on the mahogany, as shown above. What first appeared as a mistake makes sense technically. On a color wheel, the red from the chemical treatment and the green from the stain are opposite each other, producing a perfect color.

## Supplies

866-548-1677 | finishsupply.com

▶ Potassium dichromate
$11.60 per 1/2 pound

## Finish Now, Assemble Later

Before I did any assembly work, I brushed on the potassium dichromate solution and wiped each part dry. Letting the parts dry overnight, I applied the stain I had mixed, waited about five minutes and wiped off the excess. Doing all of the color work before assembly let me get an even coat on all the surfaces of all the parts. This saved me from reaching in and around the legs and rails on the assembled table base.

After letting the color coat of oil dry overnight, I assembled the table base in stages. I first glued and clamped the four pairs of outer and inner legs. After these had been in the clamps for an hour, I glued the longer center rails in between each subassembly, as shown at left. Finally I glued the four end rails between the front and back assemblies to complete the base of the table.

With the table base together, I drilled ¼"-diameter holes

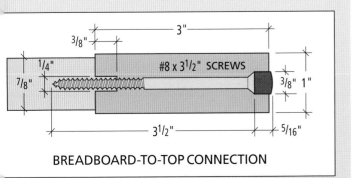

**BREADBOARD-TO-TOP CONNECTION**

*Once the coloring of the wood is complete, the table base is assembled in stages. Here I'm gluing the center rails between each subassembly.*

through the mortise-and-tenon joints in the central plugs of the outside legs. I inserted 1¼"-long dowels in each of these holes, driving the ends flush with the bottom of the square holes.

I dipped the plugs in my ebonizing solution and applied it to the visible parts of the splines with a brush. After these small parts were dry, I put a small amount of glue on the end of each plug and drove them into place, as shown at right. The splines were driven into their slots after I applied glue to the slots in the top only.

I screwed ⅞"-square cleats to the inside of the two end rails, and to the two long front and back rails so that I could attach the top to the base with screws. With 107 parts now in their proper places, I gave the entire table three additional coats of Danish oil.

Greene and Greene hold an important place in the history of American design, melding the influences of the Arts & Crafts movement with Japanese design elements in a unique way. Making this piece provided an opportunity to practice authentic detailed work. Had I been working for the Hall brothers in 1907, with a houseful of trim and many more furniture pieces to go, I would have been just warming up.

*The solution of potassium dichromate oxides the mahogany, turns it a rusty orange color and gives it an aged patina. After this treatment, a green stain made of artist's oils and Danish oil is applied.*

*A small, flat riffler is used to clean up the edges of the square holes. A slight chamfer on the back of the oversized square plugs gets them started in the holes before they are driven home with a dead-blow mallet.*

*After wiping off the excess, the mahogany is left a rich, reddish brown color. This is the same technique used in original Greene and Greene furniture. After the stain dries, three additional coats of oil are applied.*

# Greene & Greene Finish

I received an e-mail from a reader the other day, asking about finishes for Greene & Greene furniture. It's one of those areas where we have some good clues about what was used, but we can't be certain. There were some variations in color from house to house, as well as variations in wood. These pieces also lived in wealthy households, and it's quite likely that they received a regular "polishing" of some sort, and over time that can affect what we see today.

Generally speaking, mahogany was used most often, and the finishes are nice, but not overly stained or filled. For the sideboard I built for the article, I used a finish recipe that I found online at the Greene & Greene Virtual Archives. The recipe was sent to the owner of the Thorsen house by Charles Greene, apparently so that some repairs or new work could be made to match work done when the house was originally built in 1908-1910.

Charles Greene's handwritten recipe and notes are available online at the Greene & Greene Virtual Archives.

Follow this link for Charles Greene's finish recipe: (*http://dpg.lib. berkeley.edu/webdb/ggva/search?project=&siteid=259&pageno=3 &id=EDA.1959-1.III44.008&multipage=1&itemno=1*)

And this link to Charles Greene's note to William Thorsen about the finish.: (*http://dpg.lib.berkeley.edu/webdb/ggva/sear ch?project=&siteid=259&pageno=&id=EDA.1959-1.III44.009& multipage=1&itemno=1*)

# The Lost Stickley Table

## A one-of-a-kind table reappears after 100 years.

Most original Gustav Stickley furniture can be easily identified by model number. This was, after all, factory-made furniture and pieces were designed to be made in multiples. When you come across an antique, you can look it up in an old catalog to identify it. However, the only known example of this small table appeared at a Sotheby's auction in late 2004.

This uncataloged piece was likely a prototype, never put into factory production. What makes it unique is the front and back splay of the legs. It's this slight angle that gives this table more character than straight-legged versions that were mass produced. It's also the likely reason this piece never got beyond the prototype stage.

This table features many of the Stickley design elements that appear in other pieces. There isn't much material in it, but there is a good deal of labor-intensive, head-scratching joinery involved. This probably made it too expensive to be marketed at a reasonable price, but that does make it a great project on which to practice and develop joinery skills.

The anonymous cabinetmaker who built this prototype lived when it was a great time to be a woodworker. Hand-tool skills had not yet been forgotten, and machinery was in use to make life in the shop easier.

As I planned how I would make this piece, I realized it made sense to do some of the work with machine methods, while on other parts it would be quicker and easier to make some joints by hand.

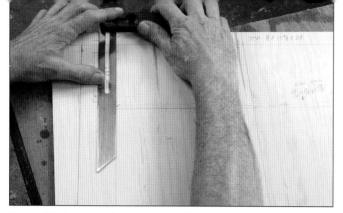

Using a full-size section drawing is essential; it lets me set angles and shows the exact sizes of parts without any of the risks of measuring.

Thin veneers tend to buckle when clamped. Gluing them in a stack applies even pressure to keep them flat.

Angled scrap

An angled block of scrap wood tilts the leg to cut an angled mortise parallel to the top of the leg.

The quick and easy way to make the angled cuts for the through tenons is with a handsaw, guided by an angled block of wood.

## First Things First

Before cutting any lumber, I made a full-size section drawing on a piece of plywood. This helped me plan the sequence of building, and the sizes of the joints. It also established a reference to the exact size and shape of the parts.

While I was building this table, I referred to this drawing rather than relying on calculations, numbers and measuring. My CAD program tells me that the angle of the legs is 3.56° and that the length of the bottom edge of the rail between the legs is $15^{17}/_{32}$". Neither of those pieces of information is needed, and trying to build to the numbers instead of referring to the full-size drawing only slows things down and invites mistakes.

I made the legs by laminating two $^{13}/_{16}$"-thick pieces together, then covering the edge seams with $\frac{1}{8}$"-thick veneer that I resawed from the same boards I used for the other parts of the legs. This is the method originally used by Gustav Stickley to show quartersawn figure on all four edges of a leg. To keep the thin pieces flat, I glued and clamped all of the legs together at one time.

After trimming the edges of the veneer flush with my smoothing plane, I cut the angles at the top and bottom of each leg. I then returned to the full-size layout to locate the mortises. The mortises in each leg are in different locations, so I marked each leg's position in the table on its top. As I made other pieces, I marked which leg they joined to with a red lumber crayon.

The mortises on the back of the front legs, and the front of the back legs are parallel to the top and bottom of the legs. I put an angled block of scrap on the bed of the hollow-chisel mortiser to make these mortises.

## The Best Made Plans

I planned on making the remaining mortises in the legs with the mortiser, but on the second mortise, the machine broke down. Faced with a deadline, I switched to plan B and made these mortises with my plunge router.

# Stickley Splayed-leg table

| NO. | ITEM | DIMENSIONS (INCHES) T | W | L | MATERIAL | COMMENTS |
|-----|------|------|------|------|----------|----------|
| 1 | Top | $^{13}/_{16}$ | $15^3/_8$ | 21 | QSWO | |
| 2 | Top aprons | $^{13}/_{16}$ | $4^1/_4$ | $17^7/_8$ | QSWO | $1^1/_4$" ATBE |
| 2 | Lower rails | $^7/_8$ | $5^1/_4$ | $13^5/_8$ | QSWO | $1^1/_4$" TBE |
| 1 | Lower stretcher | $^3/_4$ | $3^7/_8$ | $22^1/_4$ | QSWO | $1^{13}/_{16}$" BSTBE |
| 4 | Legs | $1^5/_8$ | $1^7/_8$ | 27 | QSWO | Angle both ends |
| 1 | Back apron | $^{13}/_{16}$ | $4^1/_4$ | $13^5/_8$ | QSWO | $1^1/_4$" TBE |
| 1 | Rail below drawer | $^{13}/_{16}$ | $^{13}/_{16}$ | $12^5/_8$ | QSWO | $^3/_4$" TBE |
| 1 | Drawer front | $^{13}/_{16}$ | $3^1/_2$ | $11^1/_8$ | QSWO | Bevel both edges to fit |
| 2 | Tenon keys | $^1/_2$ | $^5/_8$ | 2 | QSWO | Taper to fit through tenons |
| 2 | Drawer sides | $^5/_8$ | $3^1/_4$ | $15^7/_8$ | Maple | |
| 1 | Drawer back | $^5/_8$ | $3^1/_4$ | $11^1/_8$ | Maple | |
| 1 | Drawer bottom | $^1/_4$ | $10^1/_2$ | $15^1/_4$ | Maple | |
| 2 | Web frame stiles | $^3/_4$ | 2 | $17^1/_4$ | Poplar | Notch around legs |
| 2 | Web frame rails | $^3/_4$ | 2 | $9^3/_4$ | Poplar | $^3/_4$" TBE |
| 2 | Drawer runners | $^{11}/_{16}$ | $^9/_{16}$ | $15^3/_4$ | Maple | Fit between legs & beside drawer |
| 2 | Drawer stop | $^{11}/_{16}$ | $^9/_{16}$ | 6 | Maple | Fit behind drawer |

QSWO=quartersawn white oak; TBE=tenon both ends; BSTBE=beveled shoulder tenon both ends;

ATBE=angled tenon both ends

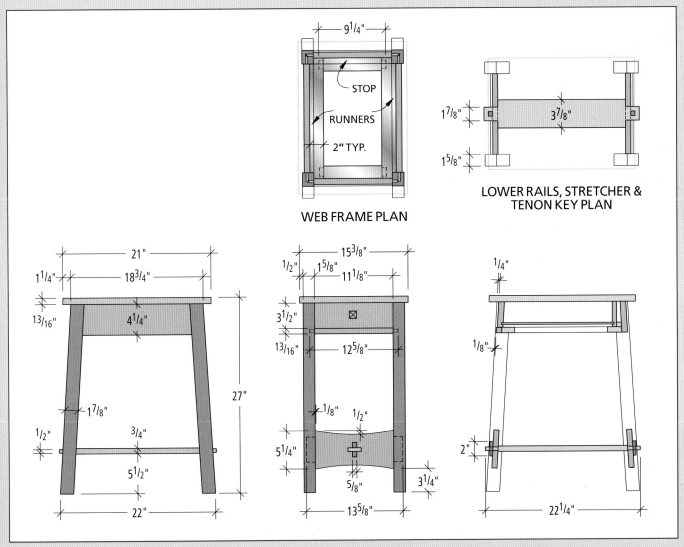

WEB FRAME PLAN

LOWER RAILS, STRETCHER & TENON KEY PLAN

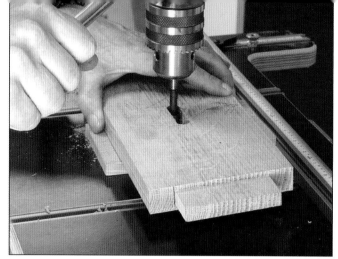

*The angled mortises on the lower rails were roughed out with a Forstner bit on the drill press. A tapered block under the workpiece makes the holes at the correct angle.*

*These angled shoulder cuts would be tricky to make with power tools.*

*After squaring the corners of the mortise with a chisel, I use a rasp to finish smoothing the inside of the angled joint.*

*After fitting the through tenon, the location of the second mortise is laid out, keeping the back of the hole just behind the face of the rail.*

The through mortises that pierce the lower front and back rails are at an angle to the face, and I'd planned to use an angled block on the bed of the mortiser to make them. Instead, I used a similar setup on the drill press. I removed most of the waste with a Forstner bit, then cleaned up the openings with chisels and rasps.

I made the straight and standard tenons on the ends of the lower rails on the table saw. I used a miter gauge to cut the tenon shoulders, and a jig that rides on the fence to cut the cheeks.

I considered making the angled cuts on the remaining tenons on the table saw, but realized each angled setup would need to be done twice: One to the right and one to the left. I decided to make a guide block that could be reversed for my handsaw, as seen in the photos at bottom left and center.

This was a quick and accurate method, and I was able to make all four saw cuts for each joint in sequence. This helped to keep the parts in order, and prevented making any miscuts by machine.

I dry-fitted the front and back legs with the top rails, and checked this assembly against my full-size layout. The angles matched, so I knew I could determine the length and angle

The mortise is cut with one plunge of the hollow-chisel mortiser. A piece of scrap below the cut supports the tenon, keeping the wood from breaking on the back side.

As the tenon key is fit, the length above and below the through tenon changes. I leave the key long and mark the length once I have a good fit.

After cutting the key to length, I round the edges above and below the completed joint.

of the lower stretcher directly from the full-size drawing. The critical length on this part is the distance between the shoulders of the through tenons. The angled parts of these tenons are short, but they need to be exact. I didn't want to risk a miscut on the table saw, so I used another angled block to guide my handsaw.

## The Key to a Good Fit

I did use the table saw tenoning jig to cut the wide cheeks of the through tenons on the lower stretcher, and the band saw to cut the edge cheeks. I made all of these cuts a hair big. Through tenons always demand some hand fitting. I used chisels, rasps and a shoulder plane to fit the tenons, checking the fit frequently as I came close to the finished size.

With the through tenons fit, there were only two mortises remaining: Those for the keys that hold the lower stretcher to the lower rails. These look difficult, but are actually the easiest joints to make in the piece. With the tenon fit in its mortise, I made a pencil mark at the intersection.

Taking the pieces back apart, I made another line slightly behind the first one. This puts the mortise just behind the intersection, and ensures that the key pulls the two lower rails tightly together. Luckily a repair part for the mortiser arrived, and I could cut these mortises with one stroke of the ½" chisel. I used a piece of scrap under the tenon to support it while the cut was made.

In most pieces with a keyed tenon, the mortise is angled slightly to allow the key to wedge in place. Because the rails are tilted back and the stretcher is horizontal, the angle of the rail allows the key to wedge in a straight mortise. To make the keys, I cut a few long pieces of scrap to slightly more than the ½" width of the mortise by ⅝". I cut pieces about 6" long, and cut the taper on the band saw. I used my block plane to remove the saw marks, and bring the keys down to a snug fit.

This method let me get a good fit without worrying about the length of the keys. When I was happy with the fit, I marked ¾" above and below the protruding tenon to get the finished length of the keys.

The last parts to be made were the narrow rail below the drawer and the web frame. The rail is thin so that it can be turned 90° to show quartersawn figure on its face. It is also beveled to be parallel with the front faces of the legs. The web frame is made from poplar, and is mortise and tenoned together. When I had all the joints fit, I made a dry assembly of the table. Then I took the pieces back apart so I could plane, scrape and sand all of them before gluing the entire table together.

I glued in stages, making subassemblies of front and back legs, and the top aprons. I cut some angled blocks and attached them to the top of the legs with masking tape so that

The assembled web frame is notched around the legs. After fitting the drawer runners between the legs, they are screwed in place, and the drawer stop is also attached with screws to the frame.

After routing most of the waste, I use a chisel to pare the pins down the rest of the way. The router quickly establishes a consistent depth.

I laid out the tails with the same angles from horizontal that I would have if the drawer front were vertical. The knob is cut with the band saw, and shaped with a rasp.

the clamps would pull straight on the angled legs.

After letting the glue dry on these, I put one of the leg assemblies flat on my bench. I put glue in the mortises, and put in the upper-back rail, the small rail below the drawer, and the lower rails, with the stretcher in place between them. I then brushed glue on the tenons, and placed the second leg assembly on top. Turning the table upright on my bench, I clamped the joints and began to worry about the drawer.

Half-blind dovetailed drawers don't bother me, but I'd never made one with the face tilted back at an angle. I decided to lay out the tails with the same angles they would have if the drawer front were vertical. This makes the top and bottom angles of the tails different in relation to the slanted drawer front which made the layout tricky, but it looked right when the joints were completed.

After cutting the tails by hand, I laid out the pins on the ends of the drawer front, and removed most of the waste with an upcut spiral bit in my trim router. This speeds things up, and gives a perfectly flat surface where the back of the tail rests on the bottom of the pin. I then used a chisel to pare down to the layout lines.

The pull was made from a cutoff piece from one of the legs. I trimmed it down to $1\frac{1}{4}$" x $1\frac{1}{4}$" by about 3" long. The pull finishes at $1\frac{1}{8}$" but the extra length gave me something to hold on to while cutting it to shape. I laid out the shape of the pull on two adjacent faces, and cut it out on the band saw. I didn't worry about the exact size of the radius below the pyramid shaped top; that would come from the shape of my rasp.

After cutting one face, I taped the scraps back on the block with clear packing tape and cut the adjacent side. With the rough cutting complete, I clamped the extra length in my vise, and finished shaping the pull with a rasp. The finished pull is held to the drawer front with a #8 x $1\frac{1}{4}$" screw from inside the drawer.

I wanted an authentic looking finish, but didn't want to go to the trouble of fuming it with ammonia. I used W.D. Lockwood Dark Fumed Oak aniline dye (wdlockwood.com or 866-293-8913) diluted with alcohol. I brushed on the dye, and wiped it with a rag. I then brushed on two coats of amber shellac. After letting the shellac dry, I attached the top with figure-eight fasteners. I took off the gloss of the shellac with a Scotch-Brite pad and applied a coat of paste wax.

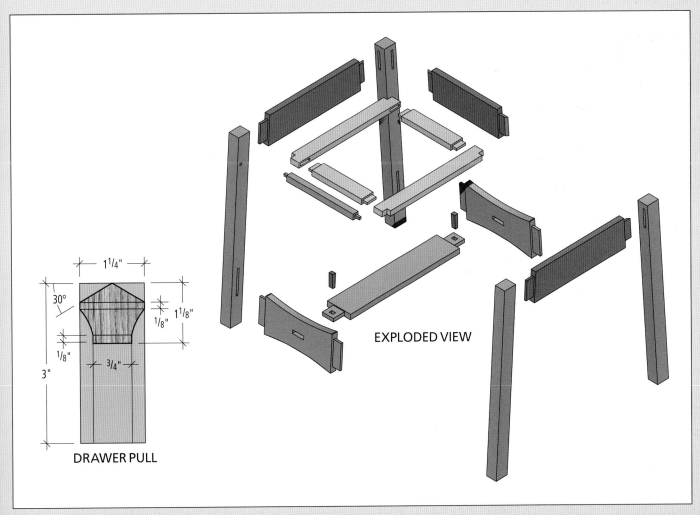

DRAWER PULL

EXPLODED VIEW

# ▶ Slanted View of Mortises

In the Stickley side table, there are enough variations of mortise and tenon joints to give your hands and your head a real workout. One of the things I enjoy most about woodworking is puzzing out how to do things. This is the top of one of the back legs. The tenons in the back rail are standard-right angles all the way around, but the side rail tenons are at an angle to match the splay of the legs. The two mortises intersect, so the ends of the tenons are beveled back to keep them from interfering with each other. The idea is to keep as much length as possible in the tenons, not to have a pretty miter joint inside the leg where no one will ever see it. I fit each tenon individually; then I take my block plane to the ends. The tenon on the back rail is straight; so I could cut the shoulders on the table saw. I was tempted to use the same method for the angle tenon on the side rail, but I didn't want to mess around with changing the angle on the fence of our sliding table back and forth between square and the angles I needed. To make the shoulder cuts on both faces of the rail, the setup would need to be reversed. That isn't impossible, but it's one of those cases where using a machine isn't the easiest, most accurate method.

Instead, I made an angled guide block to use with my Japanese-style saw. I'm using the fingers of my left hand to keep the saw tight to the block. Once the kerf is established, I don't need it there and move it out of the way. The kerf then registers the next cuts and the placement of the guide block.

After making the four shoulder cuts, I used a tenoning jig that slides on the table saw fence to cut the cheeks. I used an agled block to support the rail against the vertical fence on the jig. At the start of construction, I cut a piece of scrap to the angle of the legs from horizontal. I used it for the tenons and also under the legs when cutting the mortises for the angled tenons. My bench always looks pretty trashy because I hang on to things like this, but you never know when something might come in handy.

Here's one of the completed tenons. I aim to get a fit that can be put together by hand without beating on it that will stay together if you pick up the piece with the tenon. I usually use a shoulder plane for trimming and tuning the fit, but sometimes I use a rasp on the faces of the cheeks. A couple days after I finished fitting everything, we received some cool planemakers floats that I will use next time I do something like this.

I want the shoulders to come down tight, and the cheeks to be snug, but I leave a little room at the bottom and ends of the mortise. I tend to put things together and take them back apart as I go, and the space at the ends of the mortise lets me wiggle the joint to get it apart.

Down at the bottom of the table, there are keyed through tenons where the front to back stretcher joins the arched lower rails. Once again, I could have cut these with the table saw, but I thought it faster and more accurate to do it by hand. I used another guide block for the saw, this one was beveled to make the top and bottom shoulder cuts. Everything looks a little rough at this point, I like to fit the joints before making the parts smooth enough to finish. Pieces can get beat up during fitting, and if I make a mistake on the joint I don't have a lot of labor invested.

Most of the mortises were made with a hollow-chisel mortiser or a plunge router. I really don't have a preference between the two. I started this project intended to use the mortiser for everything but it broke down after a few mortises and I had to switch to plan B and used the router for the leg mortises. The rails were too short to clamp down and get the router

in position, so I switched to plan C, wasted most of it with a forstner bit in the drill press and finished up with chisels at the corners and the rasp for the long edges.

A couple of readers have asked how the web frame is attached inside the rails below the drawer. It's simply glued in place, it can go in either during or just after assembling the base.

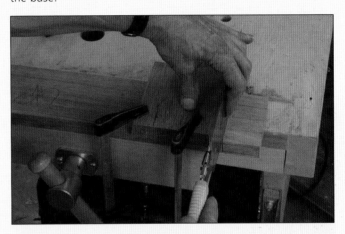

# Poppy Table

Before developing the rectilinear Craftsman style, Gustav Stickley experimented with curvaceous Art Nouveau designs.

In 1898, Gustav Stickley took a working vacation. With more than 20 years of experience as a furniture maker, he was ready to change direction, and he headed across the Atlantic Ocean for inspiration. The Arts & Crafts movement was strong in England, while in France the latest thing was L'Art Nouveau.

In 1900 Stickley debuted several new designs marketed as "New Furniture" by the Tobey company of Chicago. This table was one of the most striking of those pieces, heavily influenced by Art Nouveau and a far cry from the rectilinear designs of the Craftsman style furniture he would become best known for.

There is a hint of things to come, however. The edges of the top, shelf and legs are all sinuous curves, but the surfaces are essentially flat, and the corners are just barely broken. It also presents an interesting engineering problem. Beneath the carved surfaces and waving edges, the table is based on a pentagon, so the angles between the stretchers, shelf and five legs are at 72°, not 90°.

This "Poppy Table" has been on my to-do list for a long time, and when I came across some good photos from an auction, I decided that the time was right to go ahead.would be quicker and easier to make some joints by hand.

*Fresh look from an old design. This small tea table was originally made more than 100 years ago by Gustav Stickley. His sense of proportion and design was not limited to straight lines.*

*Following the plan. A full-size layout aids in making the parts and the joints accurately. As the table was assembled, I compared the actual pieces to the lines on the drawing.*

*The hub is the keystone. All of the structural parts of the table radiate from this small piece, so it needs to be precise. This shooting jig lets me trim it down in tiny increments.*

## Engineering First

When I began working on the design, my first concern was the shape of the pieces. I soon realized that this project would also be a structural challenge. In the original, face-grain plugs are visible on the outside of the legs, centered on the shelf. Usually this means a screw is beneath the plug, but it seemed to me that these joints needed more than a mechanical fastener.

I don't really know how the original is held together at the intersection of the leg and shelf. Loose tenons seem the obvious solution to us today, but at the time a dowel or two flanking the screw would have been more likely. I decided to use Festool Dominos for loose tenons, along with a screw to pull the assembly together. It's hard to clamp a pentagon.

At the top of the legs, stretchers seemed necessary, but it was a puzzle deciding how to connect them to the legs. There isn't any structure visible in the photo I was working from, so my solution is a best guess. I used a lapped dovetail at each end of the 2"-wide stretchers, and in the center made a five-sided hub piece that holds them all together.

## Together Twice to Make it Nice

All the parts for this table came from a single plank of mahogany about 14" wide and 12' long. I made all the joints and dry-assembled the entire table before doing any of the decorative work.

The hub is the piece I worried most about. It is like a keystone that affects the location of the other joints. Any variations in this piece and the legs would twist and throw off

the joints at the shelf. Because it was too small to safely cut on the table saw or miter saw, I cut it on the band saw. I then made a small shooting board, shown in the photo below, and trimmed the hub to size with a low-angle block plane.

I made a full-size printout of my drawing (you can purchase one for download online at *popularwoodworking.com/dec07* for $3, or create one yourself using the scale drawings on page 123) and used that to check the parts and assemblies as I made them. I cut a rabbet at each end of the stretchers with a tenoning jig on the table saw, leaving ½" thickness for the dovetails. I hand cut the dovetails and used them to lay out

*Hidden lapped dovetails. The stretchers connect to the hub and the leg with ½"-thick lapped dovetails. They are ¾" wide at the hub end and 1" wide at the leg.*

## Stickley Poppy Table

| | NO. | ITEM | DIMENSIONS (INCHES) | | | MATERIAL | COMMENTS |
|---|---|---|---|---|---|---|---|
| | | | T | W | L | | |
| ❏ | 1 | Top | $1^{3}/_{16}$ | $21^{3}/_{16}$ | $22^{5}/_{16}$ | Mahogany | |
| ❏ | 1 | Shelf | $1^{3}/_{16}$ | $16^{1}/_{16}$ | $16^{7}/_{8}$ | Mahogany | |
| ❏ | 5 | Legs | $1^{3}/_{16}$ | $4^{7}/_{8}$ | $22^{11}/_{16}$ | Mahogany | |
| ❏ | 1 | Hub | $1^{3}/_{16}$ | $3^{1}/_{16}$ | $3^{1}/_{4}$ | Mahogany | |
| ❏ | 5 | Stretchers | $1^{3}/_{16}$ | 2 | $6^{13}/_{16}$ | Mahogany | $1/2$" dovetail both ends |

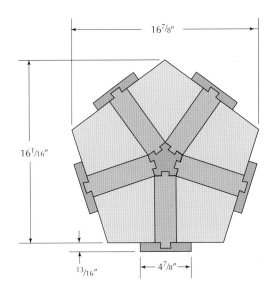

PLAN BELOW TOP

HUB PLAN

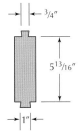

STRETCHER

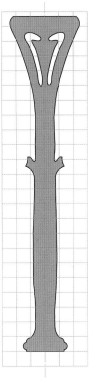

1 SQUARE = 1"

LEG PATTERN

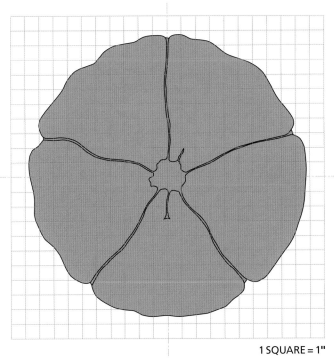

1 SQUARE = 1"

TOP PATTERN

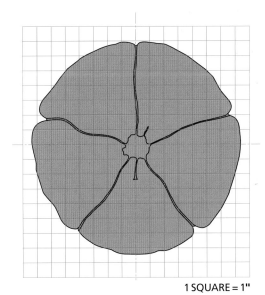

1 SQUARE = 1"

SHELF PATTERN

*Never to be seen. These joints won't show in the finished table, but they must be strong. The sockets in the legs were wasted with a small router; the sockets in the hub with wasted with a Forstner bit. I then pared them all to size with a chisel.*

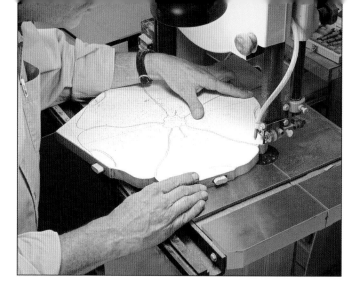

*Rapid layout. Gluing a full-size paper pattern to the shelf blank eliminates transferring the pattern. The paper will stay in place through the cutting process.*

the sockets in the hub and the top of each leg. Numbering each stretcher and its hub location helped keep the parts in order.

Because the hub was so small, I couldn't use a router to remove the waste for the sockets, so I used a Forstner bit at the drill press to establish the flat bottom of the sockets and cleaned up the sides with a chisel. For the sockets in the legs, at the other end of the stretchers, I used a ¼" spiral upcut bit in a small router with a fence to cut a smooth bottom and

back for each socket. Again, I cleaned up the corners with a chisel.

Then I dry-fit the hub to the stretchers, and test-fit the assembled hub and stretchers to the legs. After a bit of tweaking to the joints, I glued the stretchers to the hub, but left the stretcher-to-leg joints loose.

I cut the shelf to size, and made sure that it fit the perimeter of the legs and assembled top hub. I centered a Domino in each edge of the shelf at the maximum depth and at the

*Straight fitting. All the joints were made and all parts dry-assembled before doing any of the shaping to the legs and shelf.*

*Taking a stab at marking. Cutting through the pattern with the point of a knife establishes the layout lines for the carving.*

center of each leg at the minimum depth, with the top of the shelf 7⅛" above the bottom of the leg. I glued the Dominos into the shelf only, drilled a counterbored hole and drove a #8 x 1½" screw through each leg and into the tenons in the shelf.

After squaring up the shelf and legs, I was ready to cut the parts to final shape. When I was satisfied that everything was tight and square, I took it apart to cut the profiles.

## The Shape of Things

I used spray adhesive to glue full-size paper patterns to the blanks for the shelf and top. I also glued a full-size pattern to a piece of ½" Baltic birch plywood to make a template for the legs. The top and shelf were cut to shape at the band saw. Where the shelf meets the legs, I left a flat area in the curve for the joint. I ended the curves about ½" away from the intersections with the legs so I could trim right to the meeting point after the legs were shaped and smoothed.

The plywood pattern I made for the legs has the pattern on only one side. After cutting the pattern just outside the lines on the band saw, I smoothed the plywood edges back to the lines with a rasp.

I marked one side of each leg, then flipped the pattern over to mirror the outline on the vertical centerline. This saved some time in making the pattern, and it ensured that the legs would be symmetrical.

After cutting the outside shape of the legs at the band saw, I drilled holes near the ends of the cutouts, and I used a jigsaw with a narrow blade to rough-cut the shapes. I clamped the pattern to the legs, then trimmed the outside edges and the cutouts with a ¼"-diameter flush-cutting bit in a small router.

## A Little Carving

Before removing the paper pattern from the top and shelf, I traced the lines of the carving with the sharp point of my knife. After darkening these thin lines with a pencil, I used a 60° V-tool to establish the depth and sides of the lines. I followed that with a ⅛"-wide #11 gouge. The profile of the lines is mainly the profile of the U-shaped tool, so the only real challenge in carving was getting smooth, consistent lines.

The lines that define the lobes were rounded slightly at the top with a skew chisel. The central portion of the carving is slightly domed. This is the only portion of the top surface that isn't flat. After carving, I smoothed the flat surfaces of the top with a plane, following up with a scraper and #240-grit Abranet (a new abrasive on a flexible mesh-like base that's not paper. Abranet cuts fast, leaves a smooth surface and doesn't load up).

*Shape from the tool. After starting the carving with a V-tool, a deep, narrow gouge cleans up the cuts and defines the profile of the lines.*

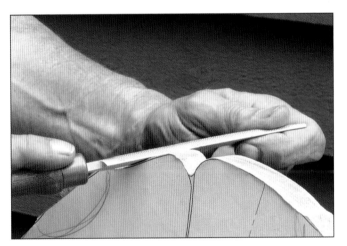

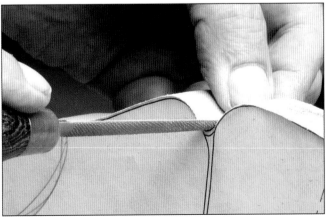

*Rasp to the rescue. The flat side of this rasp removes the band-saw marks on most of the edge. The round side gets into places the flat side can't reach. Many of the finished tight curves are defined by the shape of the tool.*

*A close scrape. The hand-stitched rasp will leave shallow, narrow grooves. A cabinet scraper follows the rasp to remove the high spots between the grooves and leaves a fine surface.*

## Living on the Edge

The band-saw marks on the edges of the top and shelf were removed with a rasp. The edges were further refined with a modeler's rasp. One of the good things about using a hand-stitched rasp is that the surface left by the tool is a series of tiny grooves. A cabinet scraper quickly removes the high spots between the grooves, leaving a smooth surface.

The corners were broken with a few strokes of the fine-cut modeler's rasp, followed by sanding with a small piece of Abranet, folded to make a slight radius. When the top and shelf were complete, it was time to move on to the edges of the legs.

Another advantage to using the rasp is the ability to use the half-round side to shape inside curves as seen in the photo below at left. Many of the curves on this piece closely matched the curve of the rasps, so I believe that the original maker likely used the same technique and tools.

I used the same procedure and sequence of tools to smooth the edges of the legs and the cutouts at the top of each leg. The router bit left a decent surface, but there were a few chatter marks on long surfaces, and some burning in the tight inside corners. I wanted these edges to be as nice as the flat surfaces so I planned on it taking awhile.

Actually it took quite awhile. Smoothing the edges of the legs took about half the time I spent on this entire project. What slowed this step down were the tight corners at the buds on the legs, plus the cutout areas. In these places, the grain direction of the mahogany changes from long grain to end grain and then back again in the span of a few inches.

No one area was difficult to smooth, but the number of curves increased the overall length of the perimeter, and each area required a different approach. I found a stool to sit on, and settled in to get it right. When I was satisfied with the rasping and scraping, I went over the entire table with Abranet to obtain a consistent, smooth surface.

## Together at Last

I made one final dry assembly, screwed the legs to the shelf, then tapped the top stretchers into the tops of the legs. I

*Final cut. After shaping the legs and the shelf, the intersection is blended with a #1 straight carving chisel. Leaving these small areas oversized until almost the end of the project resulted in crisp detail in a highly visible place.*

*It isn't cheating. The original table had face-grain plugs in the faces of the legs. It is reasonable to assume that there are screws beneath the plugs. A Domino loose tenon reinforces these joints.*

marked the intersections of the shelf and legs, and carefully carved the shelf edges down to these points.

The final assembly was quick and painless. With screws holding the legs to the shelf, and the dovetails at the top of the legs, I didn't need any clamps. After applying glue to the end grain of the mortises in the legs, I applied glue to the tenon ends in the shelf, put the legs in place then drove the screws.

After making sure the legs were square to the shelf, I applied glue to the sockets at the top of the legs, then pushed and tapped the stretchers into place. Finally, the screw holes were filled with $3/8$"-diameter mahogany plugs. After the glue in the plug holes was dry, I pared the plugs flush with the face of the leg using a $3/4$" chisel. I then went over the face of each leg with my scraper and Abranet.

At the center of each stretcher, I drilled a $3/16$"-diameter hole, and with the tabletop upside down on my bench, I lined up the assembled table base with the top. Each of the legs is centered in a lobe of the top, and the grain and pattern of the top is aligned with the shelf. In each of the five holes I drove a #8 x $1\frac{1}{4}$" washer-head screw. The holes are larger than the shanks of the screws, allowing the top to expand and contract.

I've seen original versions of this table in both mahogany and oak. Mahogany is a beautiful wood, and I wanted a finish that would show it off without filling the grain or looking polished. I used dark walnut Watco Danish oil for the first two coats and natural Watco Danish oil for the final three.

I applied the oil liberally, let it soak in for about 15 minutes, then reapplied more oil. I wet-sanded the table with a Scotch-Brite pad on the first coat, let it sit for another 10 minutes then wiped the surface dry. I waited a day between coats, then saturated the surface, allowed the oil to sit for 15 minutes, then wiped the surfaces dry.

Gustav Stickley's talent as a designer is often downplayed by those who aren't familiar with his entire career. The straight lines and masculine proportions of his Craftsman furniture can lead a person to believe that his entire body of work contains no curves or delicate shapes.

The Poppy Table was one of three similar tea tables produced in 1900. All three are exquisitely proportioned, sensitive designs based on floral forms. The style can be seen as a bridge between Art Nouveau and American Arts & Crafts. These early gems show that Gustav Stickley's tremendous talent for design was not dependent on the direction it was focused.

*First coat. Dark walnut Danish oil helps to accentuate the grain of the mahogany. Two color coats were followed by three coats of natural Danish oil.*

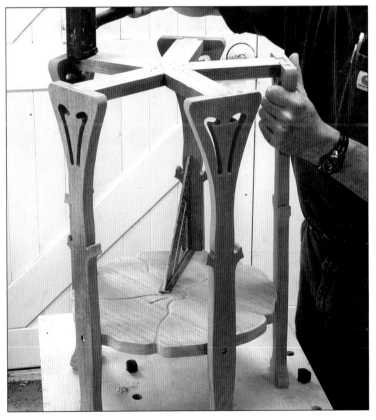

*Last tap. The assembled hub and stretchers fit into the dovetail sockets at the top of the legs. When everything is lined up, they are tapped home, completing the assembly without using clamps.*

# Living on the Edge

In every project, there is at least one process that takes much longer than expected. It doesn't matter if it's the first piece of furniture you've made or the five hundredth, somewhere between rough lumber and finished furniture is the point I call "hitting the wall." When I estimated commercial millwork projects and people asked how I figured labor hours, I told them it was simple. First, you figure out how many days something will take. Then you change days to weeks and multiply by three.

Work on the reproduction of the Gustav Stickley poppy table was moving right along when Christopher Schwarz and I had a Friday-afternoon conversation about how little tables were great projects. They don't use much material, there aren't any doors to fit or drawers to fuss with and they don't take long at all. Then he left town for a week. On Monday morning, I hit the wall.

I readily admit that I, like most woodworkers I know, am really awful about predicting how long it will take to make something. On Friday, I was on schedule: The parts were all made, the joints were cut, my first dry assembly went smoothly. Over the weekend, the carving on the tops, where I usually get bogged down, took less time than I expected, and on Monday morning, it took less than an hour to handplane and scrape all the flat surfaces to a shimmering smoothness. And then I began to work on the edges.

What I neglected to consider was that even though the table is small, the actual length around the perimeter is a long and twisting road. Getting any one area smooth was easy enough. Band saw and router marks were removed with a rasp. Rough rasp marks were removed with a smaller modeler's rasp, and a cabinet scraper and #240-grit Abranet took care of the rest. The problem was compounded by the shape of the top, shelf and legs. Each turn meant a different direction to the grain. The little buds on the legs, and the cut-outs at the top of each leg went from edge grain to end grain and back again several times in just a few inches.

I planned on a Danish oil and wax finish, and wanted the edges as smooth as the top so that the color and texture would be consistent. Each different type of grain and each transition between grain types meant a slightly different approach, or a different angle of attack. The tools that worked well in some places would not fit in others so I had to improvise with a different tool or work backward or upside down. When I put the first coat of oil on the table, I was happy with how it looked, but at the same time relieved that it was over.

The back door of our shop opens to the loading dock for our building. I like to work next to the open door for the fresh air and good light. The loading dock is also the quasi-official smoking area for the building, and the smokers like to peek

into the shop to see what's going on and to shoot the breeze. More than one asked me in the afternoon if I was still working on the same leg I had been working on in the morning. As the table got closer to completion, they became more complimentary, saying it was looking good and that I was really talented to be able to make something like that.

The ego boost felt good, but as the smokers went back to bookkeeping and planning production schedules and making calls, I trudged on around the edges. I had plenty of time to think, and I realized that talent or skill doesn't have much to do with it. What's important is keeping at it and staying consistent. Making an edge smooth is a basic woodworking task. When I was learning the trade, I was put to work making things smooth. When I had my own shop and hired someone, the new helper's main task was the same chore. It doesn't take much time or innate ability to learn to hold a tool or abrasive to the surface and push or pull until it is nice and smooth. It takes something else.

The nice sounding word for what you need is perseverance. The honest word is stubbornness. I wanted the edges and the curves of this thing to have the same buttery appearance and feel as the flat surfaces of the top and legs. Sometimes it takes a lot of tedious work to get what you want. If I deserve any kind of compliment for this little table, it's only because I stubbornly kept going long after I became bored and tired. My wife tells me I'm the most stubborn person she's ever met. I'm inclined to agree with her, after I explain to her that in my family, we identify that character trait with the word nobility.

# Hand Tools/Power Tools

When my son was in Cub Scouts, we went on field trips on Saturday mornings. One week we went to the woodshop of one of the kid's grandfathers. It was a nice two-car-garage-sized building behind his real garage; in other words, a dedicated well-equipped shop. The boys went to work on a simple shelf, and after herding the group from the band saw to the oscillating spindle sander, Grandpa decided it was time to impart some wisdom. "If you want to get anything done, use power tools. There isn't any reason to use hand tools any more. It will take you longer, and won't turn out as good." I didn't say anything at the time, but on the way home I said to my son "you realize that man is a fool don't you?" Hunter replied, "I was wondering when you were going to say something."

When he was four or five we started making stuff together: toy guns and rubber-band powered boats for the bathtub. Our main tools were a coping saw and a spokeshave , tools he could handle safely without scaring his mother half to death. One of my proudest moments as a father came when we were at a festival watching a guy build a canoe. When the demonstrator held up a spokeshave and asked if anyone knew what it was called, Hunter shouted out the name and asked the guy if he wanted him to show him how to use it. He stepped up to the bench and, reaching up almost over his head, thrilled the crowd by quickly producing a pile of shavings and a fair curve.

I've never been able to understand why people try to divide woodworkers into two opposing camps, Normites versus Neanderthals. And I can't understand why anyone would buy into that and only work with one method to the exclusion of

the other , power-tool users who will spend hours building jigs and setting up machines to avoid making one simple cut with a backsaw, or hand-tools users who claim some sort of moral superiority by chopping the waste from a dozen mortises by hand. I work with wood because I enjoy making things as well as I can. I don't have as much time in the shop available as I would like so I want to work efficiently, but I don't want to compromise the finished product. I consider myself fortunate that the men who taught me how to work with wood had a well-developed sense of when to pick up a router and when to pick up a plane.

The "Poppy" table project is an excellent example of what our publisher, Steve Shanesy, calls "blended woodworking", using power tools and hand tools together. This is a curious little table. It has five legs, which makes it an interesting engineering problem as legs and stretchers, a shelf and a top all need to solidly connect. At the same time it's an artistic expression. Every edge of the finished piece is curved, and the flat surfaces of the top and shelf are interrupted by sweeping carved curves. One of the parts, a pentagon-shaped hub that connects the legs and supports the top, is very small, but getting it the exact size and shape and fitting the joints is the keystone that holds the whole table together. This little block of wood will make the table straight and solid if it is right , or wobbly and twisted if it is less than perfect.

Because of its small size, I chose to cut the shape on the bandsaw, shoot the edges with a plane, and cut the dovetail sockets by hand. It is just too small to safely cut on the table saw and

I couldn't come up with a way to clamp it down and move a router in. I removed much of the waste in the sockets with a Forstner bit on the drill press. I could safely hold it to the drill-press table, and this made a flat reference surface at the bottom to guide the chisel. There are also dovetail sockets at the top of each leg. There, I used a small router with a fence to establish a straight back and flat bottom, and a few quick chisel cuts defined the acute corners where the circular router bit wouldn't reach.

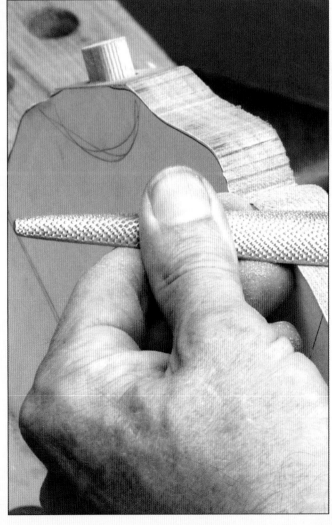

I spent a few hours over the weekend refining the curves of the top and shelf with some rasps followed by a cabinet scraper. It was a lot of fun. I worked out on the patio, enjoying some fresh air and not annoying the neighbors (at least with my woodworking). The band-saw marks disappeared rather quickly, I recognized that many of the curves matched the profile of the rounded side of the rasp, and the scraper left a very nice surface. I thought about the old man who thought power tools were the answer to everything, and wondered how he would shape this edge. Later today, I'll be shaping the legs. They've been rough cut on the band saw, and I'll use a template (shaped and refined with my rasps) and a router to make them all symmetrical and identical.

Then, I'll finish carving the top by hand, scrape the flat surfaces smooth and gently round all the edges. I'm still up in the air about that last step; I might use a router and I might use a rasp. Woodworking is like solving a puzzle. Between the raw material and a finished piece, it's all about choices: how to do this, why do that, what will create the best result in the least amount of time. If you eliminate half the options before you start, you eliminate half the fun.

# Gustav Stickley Morris Chair

## Reproduce an Arts & Crafts classic and reward yourself with the ultimate easy chair.

In Gustav Stickley's book Craftsman Homes, there is a picture of this chair with the following caption: "A big deep chair that means comfort to a tired man when he comes home after the day's work." First produced around 1906, this chair is an icon of Stickley's furniture and his philosophy.

Visually, this chair invites you to sit down and relax – a result of the sloping arms and side rails, the warmth and color of the quartersawn white oak and the upholstered seat and back. Few people who see this chair can resist the desire to sit in it. And few who sit in it can rise without regret.

Other manufacturers who knocked off Stickley's work cut corners and simplified his designs, and many woodworkers look for a way to make a chair like this with simpler joinery. Without the joinery it isn't a chair like this; it's something less. There is a reward for doing it right; in this case, the reward for the effort is the chair itself.

*Sit up straight. Or lean back and relax. This Gustav Stickley Morris chair is an icon of American furniture design with exposed joinery and solid quartersawn white oak.*

*Measure once. A full-scale drawing provides a reference for most parts of the project. It saves time, and prevents measurement and layout errors.*

*Keep your head straight. A tapered piece of scrap below the workpiece keeps the mortises oriented vertically.*

Tapered scrap

## Fools Rush In

As I prepare to build, I like to break a project down into its component parts. Each side of the base of this chair is a subassembly of two legs connected with rails. These are joined with rails front and back and are capped with the distinctive bent arms. The back of the chair is a separate unit that pivots and adjusts with a simple mechanism.

One obvious challenge is making the arm, but that is simpler than it seems. The rails and slats below the arms seem simple, but the slope that makes the chair appealing complicates these parts.

The first step in making this chair is to draw a full-size layout of the side assembly. It's a good exercise in understanding how it all goes together, and it's an indispensable reference for the actual sizes and angles of the component parts.

The top edge of the top side rail is angled, rising from a height of 1⅝₆" at the back leg to the full width of 3½" at a point ¾" behind the front leg. The bottom edge of this rail is parallel to the floor, and perpendicular to the legs. The bottom rail is a constant width, but it meets the legs at a slight angle; the back is ¾" lower than the front.

That slope makes the through-tenons on each end of the lower rail a little trickier, but the real complication is that each of the vertical slats is a different length. After drawing the full-size view, I switched gears and made the legs, which gave me something useful to do as I pondered the implications of the angled ends of the slats.

## Trees Don't Grow Like That

Quartersawn figure on all four sides of the legs was a feature of original versions of this chair, and I used the same method used in Stickley's Craftsman Workshops. Three pieces of 1³⁄₁₆"-thick material were laminated into a stack. After letting

the glue cure overnight, I dressed the surfaces on the jointer.

Then I glued a ⅛"-thick piece of quartersawn wood to the side edges of the leg laminations. These thick veneers were sliced on the band saw and cover the unattractive side grain (as well as the joint lines) on the legs. After an overnight wait for the glue to cure, the legs were dressed down to 2⅜" square.

The edges of the legs are beveled, with the bevel ending at the glue line between the solid and veneered edges. I placed the finished legs on the full-size layout to locate the tenons at the tops, and the mortises, marking the locations directly on the legs from the drawing.

I made the ⅝"-wide through-mortises with a hollow-chisel mortiser, working from both sides with a ½" chisel and bit. That size bit takes less effort to plunge into the work, and I centered the mortises by cutting one side of the joint, then flipped the workpiece so the opposite side was against the machine's fence.

I also cut the angle on the back legs, and the 1½" square tenons on the tops of all the legs before proceeding. The tenons on the ends of the side rails were cut, and I dry-fit test assemblies of the sides. I located the taper for the top rail from the test assembly and after cutting it on the band saw, I put each side assembly on top of my drawing.

## Use This to Measure That

I marked the locations of the vertical slats on the top and bottom rails, along with the mortises for the slats. Then, with a lumber crayon I marked each mortise with a number. I put each slat in position, numbered each with the crayon and marked the shoulder locations directly from the rails.

Each vertical slat is a bit longer than its neighbor, and if the slats move sideways along the rail the length will change. A slat that is slightly long or short can be moved for appearance

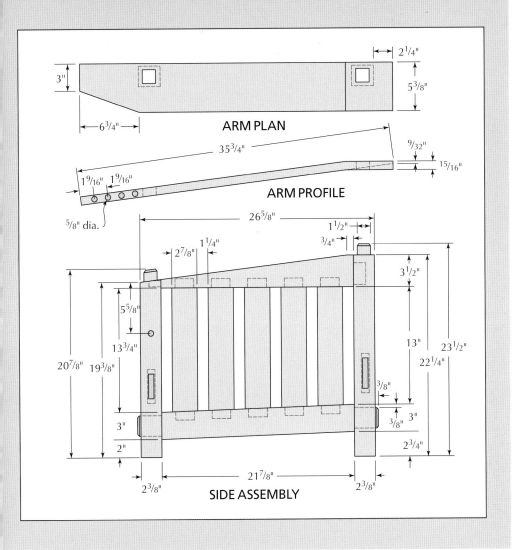

**ARM PLAN**

**ARM PROFILE**

**SIDE ASSEMBLY**

The through-tenons on the bottom rails give the chair frame strength – if they fit well. They also need to look good from the outside. Good looks are a given if the joints fit, and the key to it all is planning and patience.

The mortise walls need to be straight and consistent, so I spent some time with a float to even out rough areas left from the hollow chisel. I also made sure that the ends were square and the walls of the mortises were perpendicular to the faces of the legs. With a chisel, I cut a small bevel on the inside edge of each mortise to ease starting the tenons.

To determine the exact tenon width, I held the end of a rail against the long edge of a mortise, and made a pencil mark to transfer the width of the mortise. I then took my marking gauge and set it halfway

sake, but more than a slight adjustment will show as inconsistent gaps between the slats. Moving one slat laterally will also affect the fit of an adjacent slat.

## Many Mortises

The mortises in the rails are centered and I made them with a ³/₈"-wide chisel in the mortising machine. I saved the offcuts from the top rails and temporarily reattached them with tape to keep the mortises vertical. I cut a long wedge to hold the bottom rail at the correct angle to keep those mortises vertical.

I cut all of the tenon shoulders by hand. That gave me more control over the angles and a better cut edge than cutting them by machine. I cut the tenon cheeks on the band saw, and adjusted the fit with a shoulder plane and a float. When the slats were fit to the two rails I made a trial run of that subassembly with the legs.

I made a few minor adjustments to get a good fit everywhere. Before gluing the slats in position, I smoothed all the edges of the rails and slats with my plane and rounded all the edges slightly.

between the pencil mark and the opposite face of the rail. I made a test mark from each side and held the end of the rail to the mortise to check that the widths matched.

When I was satisfied that I had the correct size for the tenons, I marked the edges and ends of the rails with my gauge. I clamped both rails together and marked the shoulder locations at the same time to be sure they matched. The shoulder cuts are only ⅛" deep, and I cut these by hand at a bench hook using my backsaw.

At the band saw, I set the fence so that a tooth angled toward the fence was just outside the marked line. I held the rails against the fence and cut the wide cheeks back to almost the shoulder line. I measured the tenon and the mortise with dial calipers to compare the sizes. My goal was a fence setting that left the tenon barely thicker than the mortise. This prevents a sloppy tenon, but it means that some tweaking must be done to get a good fit.

Before fitting, I cut a chamfer on the end of each tenon. This makes it easy to insert the tenon for a test fit, and it keeps the end of the tenon from doing any damage to the outer edges of the mortise when it comes through.

Fitting is a matter of removing a small amount of material at a time and seeing how far the tenon will go into the mortise. I generally start with a shoulder plane, being careful not to introduce a taper in the tenon. As I get closer, I switch to a float. The float is easier to control and leaves a nicer surface.

Hatch marks made with a pencil on the tenon indicate high spots that keep the joint from going home. The graphite smears at the sticking points, and I used the float to take off the smeared spots. I don't use a mallet to try to drive the tenon in; if that much force is necessary, something is likely to break.

Hand pressure is enough, and when the tenon can be inserted about two-thirds of the way, I can look from the outside to see if there are any problem areas. The first assembly is the hardest. I usually take joints apart and put them back together several times as I'm working to tune the fit at the shoulder and to make trial runs before making a final assembly with glue and clamps.

When I was happy with the fit, I marked with a pencil where the outside of the leg lands on the exposed tenon. I cut the tenon 1/4" beyond that line, then chamfered the end of the tenon back to the line with a block plane, rasp and finally sandpaper. Leaving the line ensures that the visible intersection of the tenon and the leg looks tight.

## Bring on the Glue

Assembly of the base of the chair is done in stages; first the vertical slats are glued between the top and bottom rails for each side. I used liquid hide glue to gain some extra open time, and held the angled offcut from the top rail in place with painter's tape to keep the clamps from sliding. I used a block of soft wood and a mallet to fine-tune the lateral posi-

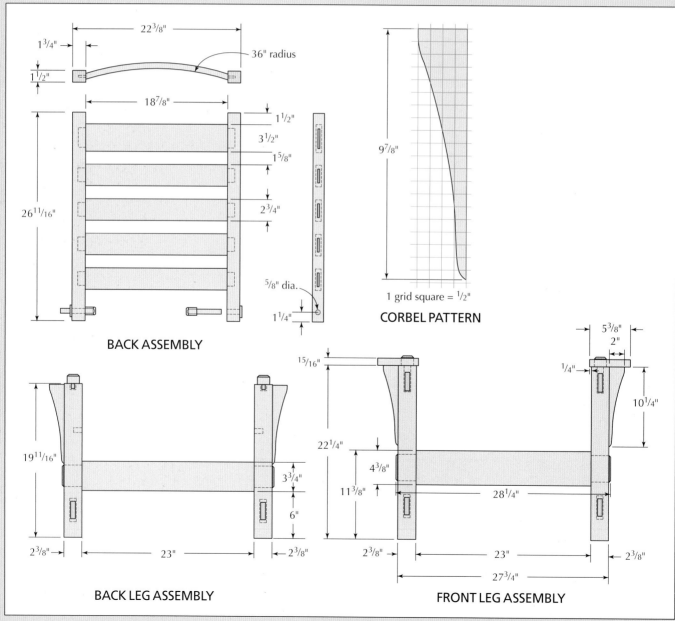

**BACK ASSEMBLY**

**CORBEL PATTERN**

1 grid square = 1/2"

**BACK LEG ASSEMBLY**

**FRONT LEG ASSEMBLY**

*Don't throw that away. The offcuts from tapering the upper rails are taped back in place to keep the clamps from sliding during assembly.*

*Only if you have to. Because the lower end of the vertical slats are angled, they only fit in one place. They can be adjusted with a tap or two.*

*Control the glue goo. Start the through-tenon in the mortise before brushing on the glue to keep the end of the tenon clean.*

*Stress management. With the sides glued into units, the last stage of the base assembly is a simple matter.*

tion of the slats.

I let that dry in the clamps overnight, and glued the legs to each end of the rail assemblies the following morning. To keep glue from going everywhere around the through-mortises, I started the tenons in the holes, then brushed glue on the cheeks before assembling and clamping the joints.

After letting the rail-to-leg joints dry overnight, I marked and drilled a ⅝"-diameter hole 1⅜" deep on the inside of each of the back legs. I then connected the two side assemblies with the front and back rails. This assembly was also left in the clamps overnight.

The arms complete the side assemblies, and are cut from a piece of 1⁵⁄₁₆" x 5⅜" stock. I started with a piece several inches longer than the finished length to get the angle of the bend and the tenon locations right first. Before making the arm, I made sure that the top edges of the top rails were in line with the shoulders on the tops of the legs.

I placed the stock of an adjustable bevel on the shoulder of the front leg, and set the blade to the slope of the rail. I transferred this angle to the edge of the arm. The bend is actually a tapered slice cut from the top of the leg, then glued to the bottom edge.

After making the cut on the band saw, I glued the wedge to the bottom of the arm. This leaves the sawn edges exposed on the top and bottom surfaces of the arm, and the previously surfaced faces glued together. I removed the saw marks with my plane.

## Location, Location, Location

The through-mortises on the arms are the most visible joints in the chair, and there aren't any magic tricks or shortcuts to the process. The mortises need to be just right, and in just the right place. I flipped the assembled base of the chair on its side so I could locate the joints in each arm directly from the tenons.

I placed the arm on top of the tenons in the legs, lining up the angle in the arm with the angle in the top rail behind the front leg. With a square I carried the edges of the tenon around both the top

*A little off the top. An angled wedge sliced off the end of the arm forms the bend.*

*Get to the bottom. The wedge is glued to the underside of the arm, smooth face to smooth face.*

*Smooth it over. Planing out the band saw marks leaves a smooth surface on the top and bottom of the arm.*

*Nothing to see here. The glue line should disappear because the grain and color are the same in both pieces.*

*Can't miss. Balance the arm on the base assembly and mark the location of both the front and back tenons without moving the arm.*

*Follow around. An adjustable bevel transfers the layout lines for the angled mortise from the top of the arm to the bottom.*

and bottom face of the arm. The procedure was roughly the same for the back tenon, except that I used an adjustable bevel to carry the lines over the edges.

When the chair is finished, the arm extends ¼" past the leg on the inside. I measured from the side of the leg to the cheek of the tenon, added the ¼" and marked the side of the mortise on the upper and lower faces of the arm. I then measured the tenon width and marked that distance on the face of the arm for the second edge of the mortise.

An accurate layout is half the battle so I stepped back and double-checked my lines before cutting. I removed most of the waste inside the lines with a ¾" Forstner bit at the drill press. For the front mortises, I placed a block of wood below the arm to support the horizontal end level while drilling.

At the back of the arm, I cut a wedge from a scrap of ⁸⁄₄ material to support the arm while drilling to keep the front and back edges of the mortises plumb. I used this same wedge to support the arm on the bench as I pared the mortise walls back to the layout lines.

I worked carefully and checked frequently to avoid over-cut-

## Supplies

**Tools for Working Wood**
toolsforworkingwood.com |
800-426-4613

▶ Aniline dye, Fumed Oak (#94) 1 oz., $7.49
*Price correct at time of publication.*

ting the mortises. It isn't possible to check the fit of the tenons one at a time. As with the through-tenons connecting the rails and legs, I beveled the ends of the tenons and hidden edges of the mortises before fitting, and used pencil marks on the tenons to locate any high spots.

When I had a good fit, I marked the top edge of the arms on the leg tenons, then removed the arms and rounded over the exposed ends of the tenons with a block plane and rasp. Before permanently attaching the arms, I drilled a series of ⅝"-diameter holes on the inside back edges for the support pins.

## Back in a Week

While waiting for the glue to dry on the base assemblies, I made the curved back slats. I built a form from four layers of ¾"-thick particle board cut to a 36" radius. I cut the curve on the first layer at the band saw, then smoothed the edge. The remaining edges were cut oversize, and each layer was added to the stack, then trimmed to the previous layer with a flush-cutting router bit.

Each slat consists of six ⅛"-thick layers. I marked a triangle on the edge of the slat blanks to keep the pieces in order, and made the cuts on the band saw. With a decent saw cut, the laminations can be glued without any further smoothing.

On the up and up. A wedge below the arm provides the proper tilt to keep the holes vertical.

Pare to plumb. The same wedge is clamped between the arm and the bench to pare down the walls of the through-mortise.

Careful comparison. Check the size frequently with calipers as you work on the mortise, and compare it to the tenon.

I used a 3" paint roller to apply yellow glue, put the stacked pieces against the form and started clamping from the middle out to each end.

I used a piece of ¼"-thick Plexiglas between the wood and the clamps to spread the pressure and prevent clamp marks on the wood, and left each stack on the form overnight. When all five slats were finished, I scraped the excess glue from the edges, ran one edge over the jointer, then trimmed the slats to width on the table saw.

To lay out the tenons on the ends of the curved pieces, I prepared a straight stick with a tenon on each end. By placing this stick on the top edge of the slats, I was able to mark the tenons on the curved parts by tracing. I then carried the lines around the slats with a square and an adjustable bevel.

I made the shoulder cuts by hand after going over the layout lines with a knife. The slats stayed put on the bench hook with the convex side of the curve on top. To cut the other side, with the curve up, I put a wedge of scrap below the slat and held the slats to the bench with a clamp while I made the cuts. I cut the cheeks at the band saw.

The ¼"-wide, 1"-deep mortises in the back stiles are centered in the thickness of the rails, and were cut with the hollow-chisel mortiser. Before assembly, I sanded all the parts for the back, chamferred the edges of the stiles and drilled the holes at the bottom of the stiles.

When assembled, the width of the back should be about ⅛" less than the distance between the arms to allow the back to adjust without interference.

## What the Holes Are For

Wooden pins serve as pivots for the back, and as stops to adjust the back to any of four positions. I started with four 1"-square blocks about 8" long and turned a ⅝"-diameter shaft on one half. These could also be made by gluing a dowel into a hole drilled in the end of a square block. I sanded the shafts to reduce the diameter slightly. These should go easily in and out of the holes in the arms and back legs.

After fitting the pins, I trimmed them to length. The bottom pins pass through the stiles of the back, and the round shafts are about 2" longer than the depth of the holes in the back legs. The upper set of pins are the same depth as the holes, and the square section should be about 2" long.

I used a block plane to chamfer the edges of the square end of the pins to an octagon shape and to round off the ends.

After the fit. Mark the intersection of the arm and the tenon with a pencil line and round the end of the tenon down to the edge. Stop just outside the line to maintain the fit between the two parts.

Work fast. Use a roller to spread glue on one side only of the laminations for the back. Keep the pieces in order and the edges will match.

Stick with it. Make a pattern on scrap to lay out the tenon locations on the curved back rails. Hold the stick in place and mark both ends without moving the stick.

Around the bend. Mark the tenons all the way around the slat with a square and an adjustable bevel. Go over the lines with a knife before cutting the shoulders with a backsaw.

Quick cheeks. A band saw is an efficient way to cut the tenon cheeks, or you can cut them by hand. Either way, cut a little wide and make the tenons fit with a shoulder plane or a float.

Round wooden washers hold the back assembly away from the legs. These are 2" in diameter, and I waited until the arms were glued to the base, and the back was assembled, to make them.

I used a piece of scrap 2" wide and 12" long, and aimed for a thickness half the difference between the back and the back legs. Then I took another 1/32" off the thickness before drilling the holes and cutting the outside to a circular shape. These doughnuts keep the back from rubbing on the arms, but they must be thin enough to allow the back to swing without binding.

The last pieces to be fabricated are the four corbels that support the outer halves of the arms at each leg. All four corbels are cut to the pattern from 1 1/8"-thick stock. The back corbels should be about 1/2" shorter in the straight section than the front. The top of the back corbels also must be angled to match the slope at the top of the back legs below the arms.

The corbels are centered on the legs and are held to the leg with glue and a screw in a plugged hole. The screw isn't necessary as the glue alone would be strong enough, but it makes it easier to hold the corbel in position. Without the screw, the corbels slide around as the clamps are tightened.

When the glue holding the corbels dried, the screw holes were filled with dowels. The through-tenons on the base assembly were also pinned with dowels, as well as the tenons in the top and bottom slats of the back assembly.

I make dowels from straight-grained scrap. I start with a piece about 3" long and split blanks from the scrap with a chisel or a stout knife. I then drive the dowels through holes in a 1/4"-thick steel dowel plate. I whittle the ends to get them started, and knock off the corners with a chisel so there is less material to remove.

The dowels are coated with glue and driven into place. After the glue has dried, the pegs are trimmed flush with a saw. The saw can leave a fraction of the plug proud of the surface, so a bit of paring with a chisel was needed in a couple places.

# Gustav Stickley Morris Chair

| | NO. | ITEM | DIMENSIONS (INCHES) | | | MATERIAL | COMMENTS |
|---|---|---|---|---|---|---|---|
| | | | T | W | L | | |
| ❏ | 2 | Front legs | $2^{3/8}$ | $2^{3/8}$ | $23^{1/2}$ | QSWO* | $1^{1/4}$ TOE** |
| ❏ | 2 | Back legs | $2^{3/8}$ | $2^{3/8}$ | $20^{7/8}$ | QSWO | $1^{1/4}$ TOE |
| ❏ | 12 | Leg laminations | $^{13/16}$ | $2^{3/8}$ | 25 | QSWO | |
| ❏ | 8 | Leg veneers | $^{1/8}$ | 3 | 25 | QSWO | |
| ❏ | 2 | Top side rail | $^{7/8}$ | $3^{1/2}$ | $24^{5/8}$ | QSWO | TBE† |
| ❏ | 2 | Bottom side rails | $^{7/8}$ | 3 | $27^{3/8}$ | QSWO | TBE |
| ❏ | 10 | Side slats | $^{5/8}$ | $2^{7/8}$ | 16 | QSWO | TBE |
| ❏ | 1 | Low front rail | $^{7/8}$ | $4^{3/8}$ | $28^{1/4}$ | QSWO | TBE |
| ❏ | 1 | Low back rail | $^{7/8}$ | $3^{3/4}$ | $28^{1/4}$ | QSWO | TBE |
| ❏ | 2 | Arms | $^{15/16}$ | $5^{3/8}$ | $35^{3/4}$ | QSWO | |
| ❏ | 4 | Corbels | $1^{1/8}$ | 2 | $9^{7/8}$ | QSWO | |
| ❏ | 2 | Doughnuts | $^{5/16}$ | 2 dia. | $9^{3/4}$ | QSWO | |
| ❏ | 2 | Pivot pins | 1 | 1 | $5^{3/4}$ | QSWO | |
| ❏ | 2 | Stop pins | 1 | 1 | $3^{3/4}$ | QSWO | |
| ❏ | 2 | Back stiles | $1^{1/2}$ | $1^{3/4}$ | $26^{11/16}$ | QSWO | |
| ❏ | 1 | Top back slat | $^{3/4}$ | $3^{1/2}$ | $21^{3/8}$ | QSWO | TBE bent lamination |
| ❏ | 4 | Back slats | $^{3/4}$ | $2^{3/4}$ | $21^{3/8}$ | QSWO | TBE bent lamination |
| ❏ | 2 | Seat cleats | $^{3/4}$ | 1 | $22^{7/8}$ | QSWO | |

*QSWO = quartersawn white oak; **TOE = tenon one end, †TBE = tenon both ends

*Turn then whittle. After turning one end of the pin, trim it to length then shave the sides to an octagon. The last step is to round the end to a hand-friendly dome shape.*

## Hard Surfaces, Soft Surfaces

As I worked, I smoothed exposed faces and edges with my planes before assembling. I also chamfered the long edges with my block plane, and I used a rasp and sandpaper to round the exposed tenons. In a few places I had some tear-out to deal with where the grain direction reversed, and I used a card scraper to smooth these troublemakers.

Each of these tools leaves a smooth surface, but with a slightly different texture. To get an even texture before finishing, I sanded the entire chair, first with #120-grit Abranet, then #180 grit. Sanding white oak to too fine a grit can polish the surface to a point where it won't absorb color evenly. If scratches from sanding aren't visible, the wood is smooth enough to dye.

I used Lockwood's Fumed Oak (#94) aniline dye dissolved in alcohol. This dries quickly as it is brushed on and doesn't raise the grain. I aimed for a consistent coat on all surfaces without running the dye. The color is close to that of white oak fumed with ammonia, and there is another similarity between the dye and fuming; the surface looks like you ruined it when it dries.

I rubbed the entire chair with an abrasive pad after letting the dye dry for a few hours, then brushed on a 50-50 mixture of clear and amber shellac. I diluted this about a third with alcohol. The following morning I went over the chair again with the abrasive pad, then brushed on a second coat of shellac. After letting the shellac cure for a week, I gave the chair a coat of Dark Watco Satin wax, applied with an abrasive pad then buffed with a cotton cloth.

I had a local upholstery shop make the cushions. The bottom cushion rests on ¾" x 1" cleats screwed to the inside of the front and back rails, 1¼" down from the top edge. The cushion consists of a solid-wood frame made of 2x4 material, ripped to 2" wide.

The corners are mitered and held together with glue and screws, with 45° corner blocks for additional strength. Rubber webbing was stapled to the top edge of the frame. The webbing covers the

*Take it for a spin. The back of the chair pivots on the lower set of pins, and the large wooden washers keep the back centered without rubbing on the arms. The upper pins support the back in one of four positions, from upright to do not disturb.*

*Suspenders and a belt. Dowels cover screws that hold the corbels to the legs. The through mortises on the legs are also pegged with dowels made from scraps. Trim them flush before finishing.*

entire opening, running in both directions in a basketweave.

A 1"-thick, 12"-square piece of high density foam was glued to the center of the webbing to give the cushion a crown. On top of this is a 4"-thick piece of high-density foam wrapped in Dacron. The fabric wraps over the foam and is stapled to the bottom of the wood frame.

The back cushion is a 2"-thick piece of soft foam wrapped twice in Dacron. The buttons in the back of this cushion help it to conform to the curve of the back, and loops of fabric hold the cushion in place on the back frame.

# Matching Mortise Size

Whenever I teach a class, at least one student will say to me "you really don't like measuring, do you?" I don't dislike measuring, but I try to avoid it whenever I can. When I'm trying to get one part to fit another, the numbers become irrelevant and measuring often becomes an opportunity to make an error. As a perfectionist I recognize that I'm not perfect, but there are some things that I, and most humans do pretty well. One of these things is dividing a space in half visually, and I stumbled across a way to take advantage of that while working on my Morris Chair. The goal here is to cut a tenon on the end of this board that will fit nicely into this mortise.

I held one face of the board against the edge of the mortise, and made a pencil mark on the other edge. This defines the

size of the finished tenon. Because I'm marking directly, I have precision without involving numbers, but I'm in the wrong place; the tenon should be centered in the board. I could measure, in fact I did with a pair of calipers. The mortise is ⅝" wide, and the board is ⅞" thick. Logic tells me I should just mark in ⅛" from each edge and start cutting. Experience tells me I would need to perfectly measure and perfectly mark four times to get it right, and if my reading or marking is off a little, I'll need to make one or more corrections. I can do that, but it will take a while.

I decided instead to take my marking gauge and set it by eye halfway in between my pencil mark and the edge of the board that gets the tenon. I'm not sure if it's because of our physical make up (two eyes, two arms, and two halves of a brain), or through human experience (my brother Jim just got the bigger half of the sandwich) but most people can accurately mark a point halfway between two other points. The shorter the distance between the points, the more precise you can be. I can barely see the 1/64" marks on my Starrett ruler, but I can easily see a point halfway between the 1/32" marks. Try this yourself and see how you do.

The proof, as my grandmother used to say, is in the pudding. I darkened the gauge lines with a pencil to make them easier to see. Here is the ready-to-cut tenon sitting on the mortise. Good layout is essential to good joinery, but it's easy to get bogged down with methods that take forever. Look for tricks to speed the process and the quality of your work will go up as your stress level goes down.

# Greene & Greene Frame

## Details shaped by hand and eye define the style.

It's easy to get caught in the trap of design by formula. But if art were simply a matter of ratios, a paint-by-number Mona Lisa would be just as good as the one hanging in the Louvre Museum. The curves and lifts that exemplify the work of Charles and Henry Greene are a good example of this.

I made this frame for a class to show how to lay out and shape typical details. The term "typical," however, doesn't really apply to Greene & Greene; each house and the furniture within share elements, but subtle differences separate them from one another. Within the style are variations.

The Gamble House Centennial

1908-2008

Greene & Greene

*Subtle differences. Elements of a style can't be reduced to simple formulas. To capture the essence of Greene & Greene, trust your eye to make the basic shapes and use hand tools to round the edges.*

*Variable curves. The radius of the rounded edges varies along the length of the edges. A series of rasps will allow you to go from rough to nearly ready in a short period of time.*

*Final slices. A curved-edge card scraper efficiently removes the marks left by the rasp and removes any high spots along the edges.*

## First, the Functional Form

In several of the homes designed by the Greenes, items as small as light switches and picture frames were included. Many of the frames have the basic design seen here: The stiles are within the rails, and the thicker rails extend past the stiles.

A mortise-and-tenon joint makes the connection at each corner, and I made the joints first. Because the rails stand proud of the stiles by ⅛", I did the layout from the back edges to keep these faces flush.

I made the mortises with a ¼" chisel in the hollow-chisel mortiser and cut the tenon shoulders by hand. I set up a fence on the band saw to cut the tenon cheeks, and adjusted the fit of the joints with my shoulder plane and a float.

With the unshaped parts dry-fit, I used a router with a rabbeting bit to form the ½"-deep by ⅜"-wide recess for the art. After routing, I squared the corners with a chisel, then marked the locations for the ¼" and ⁵⁄₁₆" square pegs to fall within each joint.

## Please Ignore the Pattern

The pattern on the next page gives the basic shapes I used, but I would encourage you to try your hand at developing your own design. Begin by making vertical centerlines on the top and bottom rails, then take several pieces of paper, cardboard or thin plywood and practice drawing.

On the bottom rail, the step is approximately ¾" vertically. Draw a line parallel to the bottom edge, and mark where the edges of the stile meet the rail – this is where the curves begin. The two radii at the end of the rail are roughly quarter circles, but don't use a compass or a template; sketch them by hand until they look good to you.

Connect the line and edge with an extended "S" shape. Sketch this shape as well, without relying on any instruments. If you don't like your first attempt, try again.

The shape at the top is similar, but the stepped line angles down about ¼" toward the outer end. The center portion is a gentle arc, and the two ends aren't vertical;

they angle in about ⅛" from bottom to top. When you're happy with the shape, transfer the pattern to the wood.

If you used paper, you can transfer the layout by rubbing the back of the paper with a No. 2 pencil in the general location of the lines. Flip the paper over, tape it to the wood and trace the lines. The graphite on the back of the paper will work like carbon paper.

## Over the Edge

The general shape is only half the battle. The edges are all rounded over, but the radii aren't consistent from edge to edge, and they vary along the edges. Before shaping, mark where the stiles land on the rails.

Start with a radius on the long edges of the stiles. Use a block plane or a rasp rather than a router. The inside edge has a small radius with the corner barely knocked off, leaving a flat of wood next to the glass. The outer edge has more of a curve, approximately ¼" at the bottom, tapering smaller to the top.

You can't taper with a router unless you make a jig. You can cut this tapered curve with your block plane in less time than it takes to find the router's wrench. Begin by making a bevel, then keep knocking off the corners until a rounded shape is formed.

A block plane can also be used for the straight edges of the rails. Be careful to stop before the pencil line that's drawn where the face of the stiles meets the edges of the rails.

A rasp will let you handle the more complex edges. The same tactics used with the plane also work here: Make a bevel, then remove the corners until a curve is formed. Remove more material at the ends as seen in the photo, then blend the shapes together.

A card scraper will remove the marks from the rasp. Follow up with some fine sandpaper to blend the flat areas into the curves, and to leave a consistent surface for finishing. I applied a few coats of Danish oil before mounting the glass and artwork. This handwork involves some effort, but the end results are worth it.

## Greene & Greene Frame

| NO. | ITEM | DIMENSIONS (INCHES) | | | MATERIAL | COMMENTS |
|---|---|---|---|---|---|---|
| | | T | W | L | | |
| ☐ 2 | Stiles | 3/4 | 2³⁄4 | 19³⁄4 | Mahogany | 1¹⁄4" TBE* |
| ☐ 1 | Top rail | 7⁄8 | 3³⁄4 | 20¹⁄2 | Mahogany | |
| ☐ 1 | Bottom rail | 7⁄8 | 3¹⁄4 | 20¹⁄2 | Mahogany | |

*\* TBE = tenon both ends*

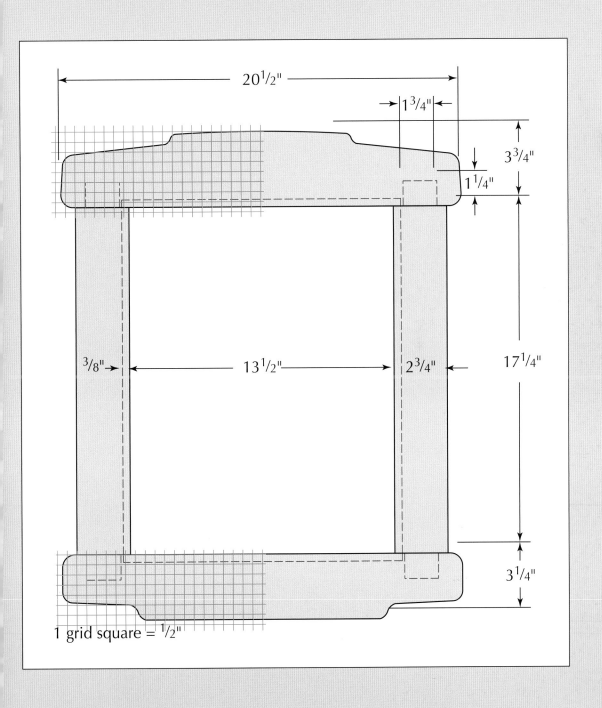

1 grid square = ¹⁄2"

# Recreating Greene & Greene

## James Ipekjian has built a career on reproducing furniture designed by Charles and Henry Greene.

James Ipekjian didn't set out to become an expert on reproducing the early 20th-century furniture designed by architects Charles and Henry Greene, and he can't really explain how he got to be where he is today.

"If there were a contest for the luckiest woodworker on the planet" he says, "I don't know if I'd win – but I think I'd be one of the finalists."

Today, he works alone in a comfortably cluttered but remarkably well-equipped shop located near the ultimate bungalows built by the Greenes in Pasadena, Calif. In the 1970s, Ipekjian was working as a model maker in the aerospace industry, and building projects from Popular Mechanics out of plywood in his garage. Bitten by the woodworking bug, he wondered if he could possibly make a living working with wood. A commission for an 18th-century highboy, as well as dissatisfaction with his job, led him to give it a try.

Working first in his garage, and later in a rented storefront, Ipekjian did all the work that came his way: kitchen cabinets, remodeling jobs and the occasional antique repair. His story isn't that different from a lot of woodworkers – except that some of the remodeling and repair work was on original Greene and Greene houses and furniture. Ipekjian had the drive to get the details exactly right, and the quality and range of his work since then has attracted attention worldwide.

*Old industrial machinery, like this massive bandsaw, shares space with impeccable reproductions of Greene and Greene furniture in Jim Ipekjian's workshop in Pasadena, Calif.*

*Much of Ipekjian's work requires detailing by hand, as in these carved table legs.*

*Not many one-man shops have a 20" jointer like this vintage machine, but then again, not many one-man shops produce work at the level of quality and detail that Jim Ipekjian does.*

In the early 1980s, Ipekjian purchased property to build a 3,000-square-foot shop. Inflation and rising interest rates kept him from building for a few years, but eventually he built the shop he works in today. He moved out for a few years to a larger shop full of old machinery, but came back to his original location three years ago when the city needed his property. For the last 13 years, Ipekjian has worked almost exclusively on reproducing the work that Peter and John Hall originally made for Greene and Greene.

Some of the vintage, industrial-size machinery made the return trip to his current shop, including an Oliver sliding table saw, one of the widest jointers I've ever seen, and an ancient yet efficient mortiser. In a small room at the back of the shop is a fully equipped machine shop. This remnant from Ipekjian's days as a model maker allows him to fabricate metal parts and hardware when he needs to.

Just inside the front door sit reproductions of two different Greene and Greene chairs, and the Gamble house's entry table. "That's my showroom," says the soft-spoken craftsman. "Nothing fancy; I think the work speaks for itself." I spent two days looking at original pieces by Greene and Greene before visiting Ipekjian's shop; to say I was impressed would be a serious understatement. Except for a lack of aged patina, his reproductions were the equal of the originals down to the smallest detail.

As Ipekjian explains the details of how a drawer was made, his enthusiasm and knowledge of his work become apparent. He actually has more years of experience working on this furniture than the original makers did. The pieces he has reconstructed range from tiny jewel-like inlays and intricate light fixtures to the timber-framed pergola of the Blacker house in Pasadena, Calif.

Ipekjian is self-taught. His earlier career gave him the ability to work precisely, and helped him to develop excellent problem-solving skills. "I enjoy the challenge of figuring it out," he

*An ancient, but accurate Oliver sliding table saw and floor-to-ceiling stacks of lumber occupy the back half of the shop.*

*These planes, including a very rare Stanley No. 164 smoothing plane, originally belonged to Charles Sumner Greene.*

## The Blacker House

Many of the homes designed and built by Charles Sumner Greene and Henry Mather Greene have suffered cruel fates. Some were torn down; others were thoughtlessly remodeled or left to rot. Before the revival of interest in the work of Greene and Greene that began in the 1970s, no one seemed to know or care what treasures these houses and their furnishings were. After the revival it was often too late to undo the damage and dispersal that had been done.

The Blacker house, in Pasadena, Calif., one of the finest examples of the Greene's worked once seemed doomed, but it is now in the middle of a happy ending to its sad story. As long as the original owner and his widow lived in the house, Henry Greene saw to it that the property was maintained, and wrote to his brother Charles in the 1930s of how good the interiors looked after being "gone over."

Shortly after Mrs. Blacker's death in the late 1940s, the five-acre site was subdivided and new houses were erected in what had been a majestic backyard garden. Much of the furniture was sold off in a yard sale, and years later reappeared in museum and private collections.

By the mid 1980s, the Blacker house looked more like an eyesore than the centerpiece of a posh neighborhood. New shingles had been placed directly over old ones, and the roof had deteriorated. Exposed rafter ends had begun to rot, and the once-colorful structure had turned a moldy looking black.

The worst blow to the house's dignity came in 1985 when the property changed hands. A new owner had purchased the house after learning that the light fixtures and art glass windows were worth more than the property itself. Immediately after closing, trucks appeared, and more than 50 exquisite wood and art-glass light fixtures were removed and sold off. The city of Pasadena passed legislation preventing the future removal of fixtures and furnishings from historic structures, and negotiated with the owner to replace art glass windows he wanted to sell with exact reproductions.

The property was sold again to an owner who wanted to restore it, but who wasn't up to the task. In 1995, the current owners began their restoration. James Ipekjian was first asked to reproduce the light fixtures that had been removed. As the restoration of the entire house proceeded, it became evident to the owners that an experienced, knowledgeable craftsman needed to be in charge, and Ipekjian oversaw the project for two years before beginning work on the lights.

With more than 50 lighting fixtures completed, Ipekjian began reproducing the original furniture. In the dining room, breakfast room and living room, most of the furniture has now been reproduced, and the remaining pieces originally made by Peter and John Hall will likely be completed in the next few years.

The Blacker house is not open to the public, except for occasional private tours. The restored interiors have been featured in several recent books. The only discernable difference between Ipekjian's reproductions and the original pieces is the patina that comes with 100 years of age.

*The renovation of the Blacker house is complete. Many of the original furniture pieces have also been reproduced, and more are planned.*

*Accurate reproductions in a corner of the shop near the entrance serve as Ipekjian's showroom.*

says, "and I'm not afraid to try things I haven't done before."

Ipekjian has spent so much time working with original pieces and drawings that he has become adept at interpreting the original drawings of Charles Greene. Pointing to one drawing he remarks, "That's his representation of a cloud; you can see it in other pieces."

On the day of my visit, Ipekjian was working on a custom table that had been drawn by Greene, but never constructed. Working from a copy of an original sketch, he was carving details in the legs. "I'm not very good at predicting how long it will take to do something. For this table, I figured the four legs would take a day, but it's taking me a day to do each one. This isn't production work; each piece is a little different," he explains.

When the Blacker house was built, there was a music cabinet in the living room that the current owners wanted reproduced. Original drawings existed, but didn't show the details of the exteriors of the upper doors – and the whereabouts of

the original was unknown. Ipekjian made his best guess, and constructed the piece. "Unfortunately," he says matter-of-factly, "a photo of the original surfaced shortly after I had this completed, and my guess was wrong. So I get to make a new pair of doors."

Getting the details exactly right has been a key element to his success, and the original pieces contained an incredible amount of intricate details that aren't readily apparent. "There's a subtlety to this furniture that you really can't get unless you've seen a lot of it up close," Ipekjian says.

His curiosity goes well beyond solving technical problems. Discussing the mechanism of a drop-front desk, Ipekjian questions where the details came from: "Did the customer ask for this, or even notice it? It could have come from the guy who made it, or Henry (Greene) may have had it all drawn out."

Ipekjian can't keep from talking about the details – how something is put together, what lies behind the detail, and what that detail does for the entire piece. He likely knows

*The Blacker house furniture reproductions, and several other Greene and Greene pieces, feature inlays of precious metals, mother of pearl, semi-precious stones and carved wood. James Ipekjian's work includes highly detailed reproductions of these incredible jewelry-like inlays.*

more about the details and construction of this furniture than anyone. Describing the techniques of Peter and John Hall, the craftsmen who built the originals, Ipekjian says, "The Halls didn't do anything the quick and easy way, but I think they were having fun, seeing what they could do."

Ipekjian's skill and attention to detail have brought him to a place that most woodworkers only dream about. He works in a pleasant space, at a comfortable pace, recreating some of the finest furniture ever made. His reputation keeps him busy. "If everything I have talked with people about comes through, I'll be busy for the next three or four years. I'm comfortable, but still I can't keep from worrying about what I'll do after that," he says.

Unfortunately for the rest of us, Ipekjian doesn't have any plans at this point to teach or write about his work, "I'm too busy really doing the work. I work a lot of hours because it's fun, and I love what I do." Pointing to a stack of lumber leaning on the wall next to some shelves he says, "You might be interested in that wood and those tools; they belonged to Charles Greene." The tools were worn from use but well cared for, and the lumber was marked with Greene's name and address from many years ago.

The tools and lumber were freely given to Ipekjian. He also has a sense of gratitude for where he is today. "I can't explain it, or possibly tell someone else how to get here, I'm fortunate to be where I am."

When studying old furniture and its makers, I often wonder what it was like at the time. Why did they do things a certain way? What were the reasons for doing this, and how was it done? James Ipekjian has spent nearly 30 years asking those questions – and discovering many of the answers – about the furniture of Greene and Greene. He remains curious and eager to find the answers to the questions he still has, and in the meantime, he has another table leg to carve.

# Coping with Curves

Time for a show of hands. Have you ever said, "I can't cut curves because I don't have a band saw, a jig saw or an oscillating spindle sander?" If so, here's a solution that involves an unsung hero of the hand-tool world, the coping saw. Coping saws offer a tremendous bang for your buck. Twelve dollars for the saw and a few more for a package of blades and you're set. At that price you don't have much of an excuse for not having one, and in addition to making curved cuts, you can use it to clean out the waste in between your dovetails.

The blade will fit with the teeth pointing either way, so you can cut on the push stroke or when you pull. I think it makes sense to cut on the pull, as that puts tension on the blade. The blades are thin and will bend, and are more likely to do that if you're pushing.

Clamp the work so it's steady, and mark your layout on both sides if you're nervous about not cutting straight. Stay outside the line and see how you do. I'm showing off here by cutting pretty close; on the other curve I chickened out and stayed farther away. Don't try to force things; watch the saw cut rather than try to make the saw cut.

It doesn't matter how raggedy your cut looks, as long as you stay outside the line. Clamp the block down to something solid and pare down the parts that stick out with the chisel held vertically. This isn't hard to do; you're only slicing off the high points. This will leave a faceted surface, and the more facets you have the closer to a fair curve you will be.

When you get close to the line, move the block so the edge is out in space and re-clamp it. To finish the curve, you want to pare downhill to the grain. To establish the curve, angle the chisel slightly so that you are only cutting a narrow portion of the width. This makes it easy to neatly follow the curve. Do this on both sides, then make paring cuts down the middle to reach the edges. In the picture above, the shaving stops about 1/16" in from the edges because I cut the edges first.

To cut the concave arc, you'll need to change the angle of the blade in relation to the frame of the saw, and you'll need to work from both ends into the middle. I never remember to change the angle until I get stuck, but you can do that first.

In an earlier post, we had one reader that was confused about instructions for cleaning up the inside arc. The block is clamped securely to the bench and the bevel of the chisel is is down. This lets me swing the chisel into the curve. The

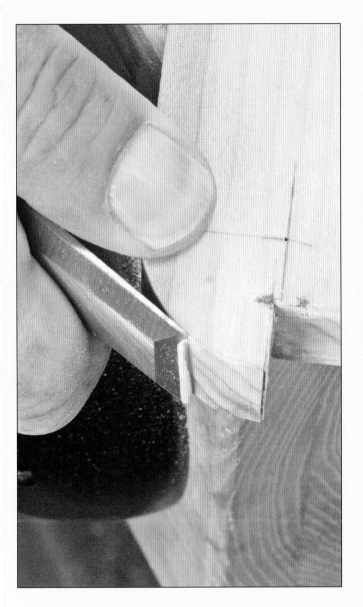

technique is much like the outside curve. I pare off the obvious
high spots and when I'm close to the line I angle the chisel
slightly to work the edges. Then I go back and pare the last
little bit off the middle. In this photo, I have my left hand
wrapped around the chisel to give more control as I make
heavy cuts.

In this photo, I'm almost done, so my left hand is now
holding the end of the chisel like a pencil. This gives more
fine control as I'm shaving off the last few bits. To prevent the
grain from lifting up, I work down along the grain from both
directions. Where the two curves intersect at the bottom of
the arc is the tricky spot. Light cuts and patience will leave a
nice looking cut.

# 3-Way Arts & Crafts Finish

I get a lot of questions about Arts Crafts style finishes. Gustav Stickley's original work was made of quartersawn white oak and fumed with ammonia. This was then topcoated with shellac, followed by dark paste wax. Gus himself gave us a good description of the process in his magazine, The Craftsman. This description is also included in the book Craftsman Homes, which is a compilation of articles from the magazine. He describes the process in great detail, but at the very end leaves us wondering when he says:

"The method we use in the Craftsman Workshops differs in many ways, for we naturally have much greater facilities for obtaining any desired effect than would be possible with the equipment of a home worker."

I didn't go into much detail in my first two books, Shop Drawings for Craftsman Furniture & More Shop Drawings for Craftsman Furniture because I thought Gus Stickley's description mentioned above was complete and with the books in black and white format we wouldn't be able to show pictures that accurately showed the colors.

My research suggests that in the first few years of production, fuming was the method used in Stickley's Craftsman Workshops, but sometime around 1906, they shifted to early forms of aniline dye stains and lacquer that was being developed by Sherwin-Williams in Cleveland. So the first question to answer if you want an "authentic" Craftsman finish is do you want the authentic fumed finish, or the authentic dyed and lacquered finish?

This is a picture of a reproduction of a Gustav Stickley No. 700 bookcase that I make for the February 2005 issue of Popular Woodworking. It's very close to the color of many original pieces I've seen, and the color was achieved by fuming. In the current Catalog of the L & JG Stickley company, this finish is referred to as "Onondaga". The reproductions made by the current Stickley company are finished just like all other factory made furniture today, it's stained and toned and lacquered. These finishes are very well done, but I don't think it's quite right to call them authentic. They look very nice and are extremely well done, but it's a modern finish with modern methods.

Here are brief descriptions of the two processes I currently use in my reproductions. The first process is fuming with ammonia. Stickley used 26% ammonia which is really strong and somewhat dangerous. If you use it, you need to read the MSDS sheet

for it. It can be hard to find. The best place I've found to look is at a local blueprint supply company, as it's used in old style blueprint machines. Household ammonia from the grocery store is about 5%. I've never had much luck with it, but it should work, given a sufficient amount of time. In between is janitorial ammonia which most hardware and janitorial supply companies carry. It's about 10% strength.

You need an airtight container to put the furniture in, and you need to expose it to the fumes for 12-48 hours. The ammonia gas reacts with tannic acid in the wood, and chemically changes the color. The amount of tannic acid wil vary from log to log and board to board, so unless you use wood from the same tree, there will likely be variations in color and in the amount of time it takes to achieve the color you want. I knock together a simple framework and cover it with plastic sheeting, tucking it underneath the frame and using spring clamps to hold the plastic tightly to the frame. I leave a flap at one end so I can pour the ammonia in a plastic container then quickly seal the end. It doesn't take much ammonia, just a few ounces. Clear plastic is best because you can see through it to judge the progress of the color. This picture is taken just after fuming for about 24 hours. When the time is up, I put on goggles, gloves and a respirator, lift up the flap and put the cover on the lid to the container with the ammonia in it. It's best to do this outside, but if you must do it inside, work close to an exterior door and use a

fan to blow the fumes outside before removing the plastic sheet from the frame. Here's a closer look at the color after fuming:

It's kind of gray and dull, but the first coat of finish will improve the look considerably. Note that the "flakes" of the quarter-sawn oak are close to the same color as the rest of the wood. An authentic finish won't "pop" the grain, it's subtle and subdued. From this point you can move on to your favorite top-coat, I like to use amber or garnet shellac as this really warms and develops the color. Here is what it looks like with a coat of shellac:

One of the problems with fuming is you can end up with uneven color, and if you miss any areas of sapwood, you can have spots with no color at all. With white oak it can be hard to tell, and this is what can happen (top, left, lower image):

This isn't good, especially if you're building it to put in a magazine that gets read by a couple hundred thousand people. Back in Gus Stickley's description of his process, he describes the fix; is a little bit of aniline dye mixed in some shellac. You can carefully blend it in with a brush or a rag. This is what it looks like in the middle of touching it up (top, right, lower image)::

With some patience and judicious work with a scotchbrite pad, you can blend it in completely before applying a final coat or two

of shellac or clear lacquer. The final color comes from dark wax, applied after letting the shellac dry for a couple of weeks.

So if you're going to all this trouble, and you risk uneven color and areas of sapwood that need to be touched up, why not just use stain or dye and avoid the fumes and the hassle? Good question. Gus Stickley's answer was to use aniline dye and avoid the fumes and hassle, once he had access to a reliable dye to use. Some of our staff like to use a gel stain, and think that General Finishes "Java" was pretty close to authentic. I think it's a bit too red and shortly after we published something mentioning it, "Java" was discontinued. They do have one called "Espresso" which looks similar. Any of the dark brown stains would also work.
I'm not wild about gel stains, and I think the sensible way to do the finish is with aniline dye. Lockwood "fumed oak" is pretty close to the look you get when you fume. I like to dissolve it in alcohol to minimize grain-raising and speed up the process. You have much better control over the color, and the dye doesn't care if the boards came from the same tree or contain any sapwood. I follow it with shellac and dark wax -the same as if it was fumed.

# About The Author

Robert W. Lang grew up in northeastern Ohio and has been a professional woodworker since the early 1970s. He learned woodworking repairing wooden boats on Lake Erie and in a large commercial shop in Cleveland. Along the way he studied industrial design at The Ohio State University, and his experience includes building custom furniture and cabinets as well as managing and engineering large architectural millwork projects.

Bob joined the staff of *Popular Woodworking Magazine* in 2004 and is Executive Editor.

He is the author of several "Shop Drawings" books about furniture and interiors of the Arts & Crafts Movement of the early 1900s.

## Metric Conversion Chart

| TO CONVERT | TO | MULTIPLY BY |
| --- | --- | --- |
| Inches | Centimeters | 2.54 |
| Centimeters | Inches | 0.4 |
| Feet | Centimeters | 30.5 |
| Centimeters | Feet | 0.03 |
| Yards | Meters | 0.9 |
| Meters | Yards | 1.1 |

Distributed in Canada by Fraser Direct
100 Armstrong Avenue
Georgetown, Ontario L7G 5S4
Canada

Distributed in the U.K. and Europe by
F&W Media International, LTD
Brunel House, Ford Close
Newton Abbot
TQ12 4PU, UK
Tel: (+44) 1626 323200
Fax: (+44) 1626 323319
E-mail: enquiries@fwmedia.com

Distributed in Australia by Capricorn Link
P.O. Box 704, Windsor, NSW 2756 Australia
Tel: (02) 4560 1600; Fax: (02) 4577 5288
Email: books@capricornlink.com.au


Visit our website at popularwoodworking.com or
our consumer website at shopwoodworking.com
for more woodworking information projects.

Other fine Popular Woodworking Books are available from your local bookstore or direct from the
publisher.


17    16    15    14    13      5   4   3   2   1

Acquisitions editor: David Thiel
Designer: Elyse Schwanke
Production coordinator: Mark Griffin

## Read This Important Safety Notice

To prevent accidents, keep safety in mind while you
work. Use the safety guards installed on power equipment; they are for your protection.

When working on power equipment, keep fingers
away from saw blades, wear safety goggles to prevent
injuries from flying wood chips and sawdust, wear hear-
ing protection and consider installing a dust vacuum to
reduce the amount of airborne sawdust in your woodshop.

Don't wear loose clothing, such as neckties or shirts
with loose sleeves, or jewelry, such as rings, necklaces
or bracelets, when working on power equipment. Tie
back long hair to prevent it from getting caught in your
equipment.

People who are sensitive to certain chemicals should
check the chemical content of any product before using
it.

Due to the variability of local conditions, construction
materials, skill levels, etc., neither the author nor Popular Woodworking Books assumes any responsibility for
any accidents, injuries, damages or other losses incurred
resulting from the material presented in this book.

The authors and editors who compiled this book have
tried to make the contents as accurate and correct as possible. Plans, illustrations, photographs and text have been
carefully checked. All instructions, plans and projects should
be carefully read, studied and understood before beginning
construction.

Prices listed for supplies and equipment were current
at the time of publication and are subject to change.

# Ideas. Instruction. Inspiration.

These and other great Popular Woodworking products are available at your local bookstore, woodworking store or online supplier.

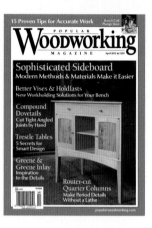

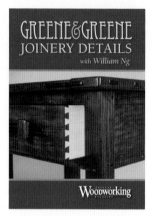

**POPULAR WOODWORKING'S ARTS & CRAFTS FURNITURE PROJECTS**
*By The Popular Woodworking Staff*
Arts & Crafts Furniture Projects focuses on popular pieces that are sure to appeal to woodworking enthusiasts of all levels. The bonus CD Rom includes additional projects not featured in the book, as well as useful tips and technique articles.

paperback · 208 pages

**ARTS & CRAFTS FURNITURE ANYONE CAN MAKE**
*By David Thiel*
Classic Arts & Crafts furniture designs are offerd as simple, screw-together projects so that anyone can build great-looking furniture. Using basic tools and home center lumber, even a first-time woodworker can successfully create a piece of furniture in a weekend.

paperback · 160 pages

**POPULAR WOODWORKING MAGAZINE**
Whether learning a new hobby or perfecting your craft, *Popular Woodworking Magazine* provides seven issues a year with the expert information you need to learn the skills, not just build the project. Find the latest issue on newsstands, or you can order online at popularwoodworking.com.

**GREENE & GREENE JOINERY DETAILS DVD**
*By William Ng*
In this DVD you will learn how to create five Greene & Green details, using jigs and simple techniques, providing a stunning finish to your next project.

Available at shopwoodworking.com DVD & Instant download

## POPULAR WOODWORKING'S VIP PROGRAM
*Get the Most Out of Woodworking!*

Join the ShopWoodworking VIP program today for the tools you need to advance your woodworking abilities. Your one-year paid renewal membership includes:

- *Popular Woodworking Magazine* (1 year/7 issue U.S. subscription — a $21.97 value)
- *Popular Woodworking Magazine* CD — Get all issues of *Popular Woodworking Magazine* from 2006 to to 2010 (a $64.95 value!)
- *The Best of Shops & Workbenches* CD — 62 articles on workbenches, shop furniture, shop organization and essential jigs and fixtures (a $15 value)

- Roubo Plate 11 Poster — A beautiful 18" x 24" reproduction of Plate 11 from Andre Roubo's 18th-century masterpiece *L'Art du Menuisier,* on heavy, cream-colored stock
- 20% Members-Only Savings on 6-Month Subscription for ShopClass OnDemand
- 10% Members-Only Savings at Shopwoodworking.com
- 10% Members-Only Savings on FULL PRICE Registration for Woodworking In America Conference (Does Not Apply with Early Bird Price)
- and more....

Visit **popularwoodworking.com** to see more woodworking information by the experts, learn about our digital subscription and sign up to receive our weekly newsletter at popularwoodworking.com/newsletters/